THE TECH SOLUTION

Creating Healthy Habits for Kids Growing Up in a Digital World

Shimi Kang, MD

VIKING

VIKING

an imprint of Penguin Canada, a division of Penguin Random House Canada Limited

Canada • USA • UK • Ireland • Australia • New Zealand • India • South Africa • China

First published 2020

Copyright © 2020 by Shimi Kang

www.penguinrandomhouse.ca

LIBRARY AND ARCHIVES CANADA CATALOGUING IN PUBLICATION

Title: The tech solution : creating healthy habits for kids growing up in a digital world / Shimi Kang.
Names: Kang, Shimi K., author.
Identifiers: Canadiana (print) 20200180401 | Canadiana (ebook) 2020018041X | ISBN 9780735239548 (hardcover) | ISBN 9780735239555 (HTML)
Subjects: LCSH: Technology and children. | LCSH: Technology and youth. | LCSH: Internet and children. | LCSH: Internet and youth. | LCSH: Computers and children. | LCSH: Child rearing.
Classification: LCC HQ784.T37 K36 2020 | DDC 649/.1—dc23

Book design by Leah Springate
Cover design by Leah Springate
Cover images: (brain) lvcandy, (squares) mrsopossum, both Getty Images; (squares) Ikrill / Shutterstock
Printed and bound in Canada

10 9 8 7 6 5 4 3 2 1

Penguin
Random House
VIKING CANADA

To my loving parents, Gian Kaur and Malkiat Singh Kang.
Thank you for guiding me towards the values of oneness,
contribution, and Chardikala. May all parents
nurture these truths in children forever.

KNOW THYSELF. LOVE THYSELF.

CONTENTS

INTRODUCTION

WHETHER I'M IN VANCOUVER, Shanghai, Auckland, or New York, I always hear the same questions: *How much screen time is okay? How can I limit the amount of technology my son is consuming? Are video games good or bad for kids? Should I give my nine-year-old an iPhone?*

In fact, I imagine that's why you picked up this book: intuitively, you may feel that digital technology has an effect on your child's behaviour and moods. Your gut is probably signalling that something isn't right—and for good reason. The warning signs are loud and clear. The more your son plays video games, for example, the more distracted, withdrawn, and irritable he seems to become. The constant exposure to her friends' portrayals of their lives on social media seems to be leaving your teenage daughter feeling down. Your fifteen-year-old's phone is constantly vibrating from notifications and alerts, but he never seems to have any friends over to the house.

Despite that, you've seen headlines assuring you that there's nothing to worry about: "Screen Time May Be No Worse for Kids Than Eating Potatoes" (*Forbes*), or "Kids Whose Parents Limited Screen Time Do Worse in College" (*Inc.*), or "Children's Social

Media Use Has 'Trivial' Effect on Happiness" (*The Guardian*).

These are just some of the conflicting messages about the impact of technology on our children. It turns out that some of the doubt and confusion is being sown by the same people selling our kids their gadgets and getting them hooked on their platforms and apps. Recently, a co-panellist speaking alongside me at a university conference argued that fears over tech's negative impact on children were being massively overblown. Her research, it turned out, was funded in part by a global wireless giant. And when word leaked, a few years ago, that Facebook was considering allowing kids under thirteen onto the network, the directors of ConnectSafely praised the move. Later, it emerged that the group was funded by none other than, you guessed it, Facebook.

And then there are the fearmongering headlines that send a very different message: "Screen Time Is Making Kids Moody, Crazy and Lazy" (*Psychology Today*), "A Dark Consensus About Screens and Kids Begins to Emerge in Silicon Valley" (*The New York Times*), "Kid's Eyesight Ruined After Parents Let Her Play on iPhone for a Year" (*New York Post*). The contradictory—and often extreme—messaging out there is enough to make anyone's head spin. No wonder parents are feeling confused!

But the effects of technology on childhood and adolescent development aren't simply "good" or "bad"; the reality is more nuanced than that. Tech can be extremely harmful to children and teens when it's used in the wrong ways, and incredibly useful if used in the right ways.

As a Harvard-trained psychiatrist with a specialty in youth addictions, I've spent the last twenty years poring over the research on health, happiness, and motivation in children. In the last decade

I've added to that focus the impact of screens on the developing mind. And I can assure you that, on the one hand, the science couldn't be clearer. The data on Generation Z—those born between 1995 and 2012—is chilling. They're less confident. They're less likely to take risks, to learn to drive, to stand up to a bully. Rates of depression and suicide among them have skyrocketed in the last decade, almost perfectly tracking the smartphone's rise. Anxiety and loneliness have hit crisis levels. Indeed, the World Health Organization is predicting that the number one health epidemic facing this generation will be loneliness. *Loneliness!* And given the sharp declines in youth mental health, the American Academy of Pediatrics is now calling for universal mental health screening at the age of twelve. So my diagnosis is one of urgency: we're raising a generation on the brink of the worst mental health crisis in recorded history.

Yet, if tech was all bad, you wouldn't see a group of committed kids launch the biggest environmental protests in history, as they did in September 2019 with the global climate strikes. You wouldn't see a group of Florida teens, survivors of a school shooting, organizing a national school walkout day to protest lax gun laws, as the students from Marjory Stoneman Douglas High School did in 2018. Without social media it wouldn't have been possible for podcaster Jay Shetty, comedian Lilly Singh, or artist Rupi Kaur to emerge, whole cloth, from social media. As your children begin to learn about podcasting, vlogging, and social media, they're acquiring the skills and the motivation to find their true voice, refine it, and broadcast it to the world.

The problem is, we don't have much time to figure out how our kids can safely interact with technology. Brain development suddenly accelerates during adolescence—at precisely the same time that screen immersion does. At that point, the frontal lobe, known as the brain's "control centre," hasn't fully matured. It's the part of the brain that asks us, *Is this really a good idea? What are the long-term consequences?* Meanwhile, young brains are wired and rewarded for risk taking, novelty seeking, peer admiration, and social connection. This intense developmental period of reward for risk, novelty, and admiration, combined with un-developed neurologic programs for long-term planning and appreciation of consequences, can make for a recipe of confu-sion, hardship, and even devastation. In addition, the dizzying pace of new apps, platforms, and devices coming onto the market makes it difficult, if not impossible, to do the research and pro-vide our teens with timely advice.

Part of our job as parents and educators is to prepare our kids for the world they're about to enter. To set them up for a lifetime of healthy eating habits, for example, we monitor their diets and help them understand the difference between good and bad foods. It's time to begin doing the same thing with tech—that is, start young, and help kids understand the link between the tech they're consuming and how they think, feel, and behave. We need to teach them that brain-boosting tech, just like brain-boosting foods, will lead to greater health and happiness. That toxic tech, including certain video games and social media platforms, can make them feel sad and anxious. And that a little bit of junk tech, whether it's a video game or a silly TV show, just like occasional junk food, won't kill them!

To know how to guide your children towards healthy, balanced technology use, it's essential to understand how kids metabolize tech—how different media and apps are getting their attention, how they're making them feel, and how they're changing their brains and behaviours. This is exactly what you'll learn in this book. And I promise, it's not as daunting as it sounds.

HOW TO USE THIS BOOK

Whether you're a parent, stepparent, grandparent, foster parent, teacher, therapist, coach, or any other significant person in a child's life, this book is for you. For simplicity's sake, I tend to rely on the word "parent" throughout, but make no mistake—I'm addressing any of you who are doing the hard, critical work of raising, supporting, and nurturing kids! Although the science of, and practices for, optimizing the human brain presented in this book are universal to any age group, I focus particularly on the period between birth and young adulthood up to age twenty-five. This is the scientifically identified period of peak brain development, with dramatic changes occurring during puberty. Sometimes, for example when I'm talking about video games or social media, you might find that my advice is tailored to children in their preteen and teen years. Other times you might find that some of the solutions are aimed at a younger age group. But that shouldn't ever stop you from tailoring my suggestions to suit your child and the stage they're in. You know best how to talk to your child, how to adjust the conversation as they grow and change. The suggestions in this book are meant to be building blocks, so you'll get the best results if you continue to work with your child and build on these suggestions year after year.

In the following pages I'll simplify the neuroscientific foundation for *The Tech Solution* and give you a variety of strategies to guide your child towards it. My goal is to equip you with the knowledge you can use to steer your child away from technology that leaves them feeling stressed, grumpy, addicted, anxious, and depressed and towards a healthier tech diet that will boost their creativity, health, happiness, and connection with others.

As I like to remind parents, we don't need to fear technology's potential to harm our children. Indeed, if you follow the solutions outlined in this book, your kids will learn to use tech in healthy, empowering ways that will help them adapt to whatever life throws their way. As we learned during the COVID-19 pandemic, healthy tech use can be a crucial part of thriving in our modern world.

Chapter 1 introduces the science of how technology is impacting the developing brain, with implications for children's health, behaviours, and character traits. *Chapter 2* explores how habits established in childhood lay the foundation for your children's future behaviours. I explain how important it is to take advantage of their formative years to guide them towards establishing the healthiest habits you can.

Chapter 3 is where we start to unpack how, precisely, technology is affecting our children's brains and how we can work to manage those effects. Here we'll investigate the ways video games, social media, gadgets, and apps are engineered to keep young brains glued to their screens by finding ways to reward them with hits of dopamine. But in equipping you with an understanding of how addiction and reward cycles work, I can teach you to help protect your children from addictive tech. *Chapter 4* delves into the dangers of screens on the developing brain. I expose the many ways technology is triggering toxic levels of stress and anxiety in children by prompting release of the hormone cortisol. You'll understand the stress response and how to recognize it in your child, and learn ways to guide your child towards positive coping skills.

The effects of technology, however, aren't all bad, and when used in the right ways, technology can be beneficial. In *Chapter 5* we learn how to help our kids improve their mental, physical, and spiritual health. Fitness trackers, gratitude apps, and music playlists are part of the answer. But we also need to push them to make changes to their offline routines. *Chapter 6* explores the fundamental human need to bond and the exciting ways tech can help kids connect and even reverse frightening new trends in teen loneliness and depression. In *Chapter 7* we learn how tech can help kids feed their talents, foster creativity, and find their purpose through developing their identities and individual talents.

Then, having covered how tech is impacting your child's emotions and behaviour, I pull it all together in *Chapter 8* to provide you with a practical six-step plan for tackling the most important parenting issue of our time. Finally, we look ahead in *Chapter 9* and consider how to equip kids to thrive in an era of digital disruption. This means teaching them to think critically and to be conscious and adaptive.

In this way, you will deepen your understanding of how the technology your children are consuming affects them and learn how to establish a healthy tech diet for your family. The key to thriving in a digital world is to *know ourselves*. And I mean *really* know ourselves—how our human bodies and minds actually work. What makes us happy, stressed, desperate, elated. That knowledge will help us take care of ourselves in a new, powerful way and teach our children to do the same. And from this place of knowing and loving we can unleash a new energy of creativity, joy, and fulfillment for our children and ourselves. *The Tech Solution* provides the framework, neuroscience, and guidance for this process. Just as a small seed grows into a giant oak tree, there is the potential in all of us to grow and flourish. And in this ever-changing modern world, our relationship with technology will be a key aspect of that growth.

1

DISRUPTION: How Technology Is Affecting Your Child's Brain and Behaviour

God only knows what it's doing to our children's brains.
—Sean Parker, founding president of Facebook

I WAS OUT FOR DINNER with my family when I noticed a familiar but unsettling scene. First it was the sweet young couple next to us who pulled out their smartphones before even scanning the menu. Throughout the meal they kept returning to their phones.

Still, they were far more engaged than a nearby family of three. Father and son seemed to spend more time on their digital devices than they did listening or talking, leaving Mom mostly alone with her thoughts. And a little way off, even a curly-haired toddler in overalls was hunched over a tablet—her parent's, or perhaps even her own. A perfect coda to the evening came just before we left, when a teenager, walking with his eyes glued to his phone, crashed into a waiter.

Don't get me wrong: I'm no Luddite; I love tech. My phone is my research assistant, my camera, my meditation teacher. It gets me to meetings on time and reminds me to call the kids' dentist.

It even encourages me to take steps when I've been sitting for too long! But I also love powering it down and going for a walk with my husband, reading a good book, or having an uninterrupted night out with my family.

From restaurants to bedrooms to cars to classrooms, screens have become an ineluctable part of life for most people. Back in the halcyon days of our romance with screens, we thought our smartphones could do no wrong. We greeted each new app, whether it was Uber, Candy Crush, Tinder, or Instagram, with gushing excitement, dutifully downloading it to our phones. But we know better now. These new tools aren't nearly as innocent as they once seemed. Not having read the fine print, we didn't realize that most of them were hoovering up our data and following us all over the internet. We know now that technology is often manipulating our decisions, dictating how we behave and how we feel. We also know that scientists are recording measurable changes in the brains of babies exposed to excessive screen time.

According to the 2017 "Stress in America" survey, compiled by the American Psychological Association, 48 percent of parents say that regulating their child's screen time is a constant battle. Fifty-eight percent say they worry about the influence of social media on their child's physical and mental health. We're concerned for our children, and we know that our own current relationship with tech is unsustainable. And yet, as we allow our smartphones to control more and more of how we spend our time, how we feel, and how we act, too many of us are letting our kids follow us down the same path.

Phone obsession is now so common that it's acquired its own lexicon. All around us at the restaurant that night, people were *phubbing* (phone + snubbing) their loved ones. *Technoference* (technology + interference) was keeping the toddler—who was glued to her iPad—from hearing her mother until Mom lost her temper. And the teen who bowled over the server is what's known as a *smombie*—a *smartphone zombie*. To the Chinese, he's a member of the "bowed head tribe"—pedestrians who insist on texting and playing games while walking. To keep them safe, officials have even built separated lanes for them in the Chinese cities of Chongqing and Xian.

Before we left the restaurant, our server stopped us to say how nice it was to see our three kids actually talking to their parents throughout the meal. She couldn't remember the last time she'd seen that. Normally, she said, kids and parents are focused on their screens. I felt a creeping worry come over me when I heard that. But I wasn't surprised.

HOW IS TECHNOLOGY AFFECTING OUR KIDS?

Smombie lanes may seem a bit extreme, but at this point most teenagers are checking their phones 150 times per day—that is, once every six minutes. Add it all up and they're spending more than seven hours a day looking at their smartphones—and that's outside of school or homework! As New York University marketing professor Adam Alter points out, this means that over the course of their lives our kids are going to spend at least seven years immersed in their phones. Let that sink in for a minute: Seven. Freaking. Years. And given the increasing pace of use, I think it will probably end up being a lot more than that.

The way our kids are using tech, and indeed being encouraged to use it—mindlessly scrolling through bottomless feeds while cycling through four or five open apps, the basketball game on in the background—is clearly not healthy for their developing minds. It means their brains are always on the go, which in turn makes them reactive and jumpy and leads to feelings of being unsettled and anxious. And with a smartphone at the tips of their fingers, many of them have never had to remember anything, or come up with a new idea, or figure out how to stave off boredom, or learn to sit and relax and just be.

New research is even showing that smartphones and screens could be changing the structure and function of children's brains. In one particularly alarming 2019 study, published in the journal *JAMA Pediatrics*, brain scans revealed that toddlers who spent more time in front of screens had lower myelination, or "white matter integrity," in their brains. Further testing showed they had lower literacy and language skills.

Myelin (often called white matter because of its whitish colour) is an insulating layer of fat that forms around the nerves. Like the insulation surrounding electrical wiring, it protects the neuron and helps nerve signals (electrical impulses) fire faster and more accurately. At around eighteen months, the neural pathway connecting Broca's area and Wernicke's area—two key cortical areas known for the production and comprehension of human language, respectively—becomes fully myelinated. That's what allows toddlers to go from being able to understand words to being able to say them, and explains the results of the 2019 study.

The importance of myelin in language development is just one example among many. The reality is that a child's entire cognitive function depends on the integrity of the myelin structure in their brains. By that I mean that their ability to store, retrieve, and process information into thinking, feeling, and behaving depends on how well organized their nerves are and how thick the myelin sheath surrounding them is. When the myelin sheath gets too thin or is damaged, nerves will not fire normally. The impulses can slow down and even stop, causing mental health, behavioural, and neurological problems.

Technology use carries with it myriad other potential consequences—among them cyberbullying, sleep deprivation, poor posture, back and neck pain, sedentary behaviours, obesity, loneliness, diminished eyesight, anxiety, depression, body image disturbance, and addiction. All of these are changing children in elemental ways, interrupting rudimental biological drives to connect, to become independent, even to procreate.

DO THEY KNOW SOMETHING WE DON'T?

Tech executives were the first to recognize the problem more than a decade ago. Shortly after the iPad's 2010 release, Apple founder Steve Jobs was asked by *The New York Times* what his children thought of the new device. Jobs told reporter Nick Bilton that they hadn't used it, that he and his wife "limit how much technology the kids use at home." Bilton was so astonished that he went on to interview a series of Silicon Valley executives—most of whom, he discovered, either barred or strictly limited their kids' access to tech. "Tech CEOs," Bilton concluded, "seem to know something that the rest of us don't." Apple CEO Tim Cook recently said that he banned his nephew from social media. Microsoft founder Bill Gates refused to let his kids have smartphones until they were fourteen. His wife, Melinda, now says that she wishes they'd waited longer.

Just how did our children become slaves to the devices that were supposed to free us, to connect us, to give us more time to experience life and the people we love? As it turns out, by design. At some point the goal of a lot of technology companies seemed to stop being about connecting people. It became a race for who could come up with the most enticing notification, the most ingenious way of getting us to check our phones again and again.

This is the driving force behind technology's "attention economy": that free app or social network or search engine that appears to have been created to help you is actually meant to capture your data, which can then be packaged and sold to somebody else. This is now a trillion-dollar-a-year industry. The data it gleans recently surpassed oil in value, becoming the most valuable asset on earth.

The human cost of all this is enormous. Your kids' devices are stealing their time, devouring years of their lives in little parcels. Every hour they spend in front of a screen is an hour they could have spent running about and interacting with kids their age or observing and learning from what exists around them—real-world interactions that are critical to healthy physical and social development.

Perhaps more worryingly, they're not necessarily living their lives the way they want to. For if they're not aware of how tech is influencing them, they risk allowing tech to manage their behaviour. It's important to consider: are they using technology or is technology using them?

Like the denizens of Silicon Valley C-suites, I've been an early witness to tech's dark side. Parents will sometimes bring their sons to see me because they've given up on school, sports, and their families to play video games. I've treated many teenage girls who reacted to parent-imposed limits on social media with threats of violence, running away from home, cutting, and suicide. The police called me once to see a boy who'd locked his mother in a basement for three days so that he could play a new video game unimpeded.

These parents felt ashamed. They felt helpless and overwhelmed. Unfortunately, though, such problems are becoming increasingly common, harming more and more families around the world.

WHY KIDS FEEL THE WAY THEY DO

Whether a mean comment is made on Snapchat or a bully is pinning a child against a locker, the brain will automatically react to a real or perceived threat in exactly the same way. It triggers the biological freeze, fight, or flight response, which is meant to prepare your body for an attack. You know the one—the hammering heart, racing blood, and narrowed focus.

What I'm trying to explain is that what your child feels in a given moment may not depend on whether a situation is occurring onscreen or off. Rather, it depends on which *neurochemical* is triggered by an experience. Dopamine, cortisol, endorphins, oxytocin, and serotonin—often referred to as the body's "chemical messengers"—are five key neurochemicals that regulate your children's lives, making them feel energetic or unmotivated, connected or lonely, happy or unhappy, engaged or withdrawn from life. They exist in every human, and trigger responses that are as certain as the rising of the sun. And by understanding them we can help our kids learn to fire and wire healthy habits that will leave them feeling content, valued, empowered, loved.

Let's explore these five neurochemicals in a bit more detail. As you read the descriptions below, try to imagine how it might feel if these neurochemicals were way out of balance. What might the consequences be for our bodies, minds, and society if the very building blocks of human health were targeted, manipulated, and dysregulated?

1. **Dopamine** drives our motivation, rewarding us with an immediate sense of pleasure. It's mainly released by activities that promote species survival, such as hunting, gathering, and bonding. And since we're no longer living as prehistoric humans did, hunting could include levelling up in a video game while gathering and bonding could involve collecting social media likes.

2. **Cortisol** and the stress response produce feelings of being under attack. When danger arises, they urge us to do something—whether it's freeze, fight, or flight—in order to escape. This causes our heart rate and blood pressure to spike. Over time it can lead to sleep impairment, weight gain, intestinal problems, suppression of the immune system, and an interruption in bone formation.

3. **Endorphins** produce feelings of peace, calm, bliss, or euphoria. They're released through activities like cardiovascular exercise, laughter, and intimacy, all of which counteract feelings of anxiety, stress, and pain. Endorphins provide relief from life's hardships, freeing us to try new things and innovate.

4. **Oxytocin** produces feelings of being safe and loved. It is released during shared social experiences, when we receive social recognition and experience bonding and intimacy. Oxytocin motivates us to trust and help others, to seek companionship, to learn to love.

5. **Serotonin** produces feelings of contentment, happiness, and pride. It is released during physical activity, positive social interactions, sunlight exposure, and when you're doing an activity you love. Serotonin motivates us to try new things, to innovate, to gain respect from others.

As you've no doubt observed in your own home, iPhones, online gaming, and social media are literally changing children's minds by causing them to release certain neurochemicals. Sometimes this has positive effects—when your kids Skype with Grandma, for example, it helps them feel bonded and connected with her. But some tech is creating low-value, high-volume neurochemical reward cycles and altering the architecture of developing brains, wiring them to want more from their devices and less from the physical world surrounding them.

Too much screen time can produce:

- An excretion of unhealthy amounts of cortisol, which triggers the stress reaction
- A craving for harmful amounts of dopamine, which can lead to addiction
- A reduction in the natural release of oxytocin, serotonin, and endorphins, which are key to long-term health, happiness, and success

The release of these neurochemicals is largely governed by four tiny brain structures—the hippocampus, amygdala, pituitary gland, and hypothalamus—collectively known as the limbic system. And it's this system that generates and controls our emotional responses.

For example, even though some tech gives children an immediate rush of pleasure, that rush doesn't always lead to happiness. Casual gaming will give your child a hit of dopamine. But too much dopamine (or pleasure) at the expense of oxytocin (or bonding) will leave a child feeling lonely, anxious, and depressed. To counteract those feelings, they'll want to get another hit of dopamine. This is why dopamine is the key neurochemical behind addiction. Social media "likes" provide dopamine too. But when we compare ourselves negatively to others we also trigger the release of stress hormones.

In the following chapters we'll explore the links between neurochemicals and your child's motivation, behaviours, vitality, creativity, and happiness. We'll also consider the brain chemicals causing your children to feel happy, stressed out, creative, or inspired when they interact with tech.

I firmly believe that tech can occupy a healthy space in your child's life. An encouraging text from a parent can turn around a tough day. A Facebook post about wildfires in Australia might raise awareness and inspire your child to think beyond their own little world. Overall, then, it wouldn't be reasonable to categorize digital media as either wholly good or wholly bad.

But wouldn't it be great if you could show your kids how to activate their empowering neurochemicals, both online and in their day-to-day lives? That's exactly what I'm going to teach you to do.

Let's remember that we've been here before. This isn't the first time parents have had to sort out how to teach children to use powerful new technologies. Nor is it the first time that human innovation has changed everything.

THE POWER OF FIRE

While parenting in the age of digital disruption often feels stressful and new, it's not all that different from living through some of the many major shifts that have occurred over time. Consider the discovery of fire, which represented a watershed movement in human evolutionary history. Fire gave us light and warmth. By chasing off bears, big cats, and other nocturnal predators, it allowed *Homo erectus*, our direct human ancestor and the earliest known fire starter, to come down from the trees and sleep safely on the ground. By bringing people together in one place to eat and keep warm, fire bonded us together, giving rise to storytelling traditions and laying the groundwork for human society.

But cooking may be the most important gift of all. Ridding foods of parasites and bacteria sharply reduced mortality rates and dramatically extended lifetimes. And given that our primate ancestors spent most of their days gnawing through roots, leaves, berries, and bark just to get enough calories to stay alive, cooking proved revolutionary. Food that's been cooked reduced the time and energy wasted in eating and digesting, allowing hominids to put their internal energy to better use: from powering their gut to powering their brain. (Even at rest, the human mind consumes 25 percent of our energy.) This led to explosive brain growth and, ultimately, the most advanced nervous system the planet has ever known. With more than a hundred billion neurons, that system processes our every thought, action, and reaction. In short, it was fire that allowed us to leapfrog to the next phase of evolution—to become the sophisticated, intelligent, compassionate, creative beings we can be today.

THE FIRE OF OUR TIME

It's no exaggeration to say that the technological innovations being developed in Silicon Valley and beyond are proving to be similarly transformative for humankind. Technology has allowed us to sequence the human genome and find viable replacements for fossil fuels. Soon it may even help us reach Mars, and it could determine our next evolutionary step.

But progress is a messy business. Tech, like fire, has the power to destroy us. I'm sure hominid moms and dads had mixed feelings about allowing their kids to handle fire. But they also knew that mastering it was key to their success and survival. So I imagine that they took their children to blackened fields to show them how wildfires, if not contained, could rage uncontrolled on the dry savannah, swallowing people, animals, and primitive villages whole. That they explained how flames could sear their lungs if they stood too close. That they taught them how to use rocks to spark fires of their own.

Parents today face a similar quandary: we know that our children's success will require them to master multiple technologies, and yet we fear the risk. But we can't bury our heads in the sand, let them set their own rules, and pray that they somehow avoid seeing the most graphic, violent porn, for example. Nor can we simply bar our kids from ever playing *Grand Theft Auto* or opening an Instagram account. They need our help steering them towards healthy screen time and away from the apps and video games that trigger stress and cause them to retreat into their own worlds online. We need to take them out onto the savannah.

We need to explain how the constant exposure to their friends' portrayals of their lives can make them feel inadequate, especially in moments when they're already feeling down. That it can inhibit their academic performance and their ability to make friends. That the more dependent they become on likes, retweets, and reshares, the more distracted, anxious, and depressed they risk becoming. They need to understand how easily they can be bullied online and how readily they can become addicted to their phones and video games.

DON'T FREAK OUT

But let's not overthink this. *The New York Times* recently reported that some families have begun hiring coaches to help them raise phone-free children—"screen consultants" who remind parents how people raised children before the advent of the smartphone. The *Times* piece almost reads as a Bay Area parody. Trust me on this: you don't need a screen coach.

I'm going to provide you with the best and the latest neuroscience and explain in simple terms how your kids' brains and nervous systems work and how success happens. Once you truly understand how tech is making your children feel, we can apply the analogy of healthy eating to screen time, offering you a familiar, digestible plan for the most important parenting issue of our era.

Keep in mind that the smartphone has been with us for only a decade and a half. That's why this feels so confusing. Although you may not see it, we're living in an era of disruption. It's not natural for us to be indoors, all alone, hunched over and staring at our screens all day long. For ten thousand years we were agrarian; we spent our days outdoors, working side by side. For about seventy thousand years before that we were hunter-gatherers and lived in tribes. We slept when the sun went down. We woke when it rose. We were moving all day long, and we were exquisitely connected to nature and to each other.

But don't worry: we can go back to who we are. It doesn't matter what tech keeps coming—and believe me, it's going to keep coming—since who we are as humans fundamentally isn't going to change.

I believe in science. I believe in research. I believe in raising children who are smart, happy, and strong and can reach their highest potential. And I think most things are reasonable in moderation. My guiding principle when it comes to all things tech is to not freak out and to use intuition as a guide. Breathe. We're going to get through this together.

REMEMBER . . .

- Most teenagers check their phones 150 times per day, making them reactive and jumpy and leading to feelings of being unsettled and anxious.
- Smartphones and screens could be changing the structure and function of children's brains.
- All of this is changing children in elemental ways, interrupting rudimental biological drives to connect, to become independent, even to procreate.
- What a child feels in a given moment depends on which neuro-chemical is triggered by an experience.
- Dopamine drives our motivation, rewarding us with an immediate sense of pleasure.
- Cortisol and the stress response produce feelings of being under attack.
- Endorphins produce feelings of peace, calm, bliss, or euphoria.
- Oxytocin produces feelings of being safe and loved.
- Serotonin produces feelings of contentment, happiness, confidence, and self-respect.

2

PATHWAYS: The Power of Habits in Helping Your Child Reach Their Full Potential

We are what we repeatedly do. Excellence, then, is not an act, but a habit.

—ARISTOTLE

WHEN I WAS PREGNANT with my first child, I thought I was reasonably well prepared for motherhood. I was thirty-three at the time and a medical doctor who'd worked closely with postpartum mothers, children, and families for several years. I'd helped my four older siblings with their babies, children, and teens. I'd read all the classic parenting books and subscribed to all the new rage blogs. When our beautiful boy named Joesh was born, I was completely overjoyed and overwhelmed.

I became a mom in 2005, the year the population of the internet reached one billion. At times it felt as if everything I needed to know could be found online. At other times I felt overloaded with information and contradictory nonsense. Technology was everywhere, and the promise it heralded felt immense. I was given the entire Baby Einstein DVD series and played them all for Joesh, hoping some of the "Einstein" would rub off!

At around twelve months, Joesh's weight began dropping significantly. Every week it dropped further; he went from the eighty-fifth to below the fifth percentile for his age. My happy, chubby baby had essentially stopped eating. At feeding time he'd purse his lips tight and bend his neck and face as far away as he could. I took him to doctors, specialists, the nutrition program at our local children's hospital. No one could give us answers other than "He won't likely let himself starve, so keep trying to get a spoon in whenever you can." So we tried everything: singing, puppets, every possible food combination. Some days our kitchen felt like a full-blown circus as we struggled to get Joesh to take even a few spoonfuls. It was stressful and exhausting.

Then one day his older cousins had come over and were watching the movie *Finding Nemo*. Joesh was mesmerized. When he saw the talking shark his jaw dropped, at which point I shoved some puréed yams into his mouth. Entranced by the film, he swallowed them! I popped in a few more heaping spoonfuls, and it was like a miracle: down they went. For once we didn't need a full-on Broadway production just to get half a mushed banana into him. With just a few minutes of Disney, my child was nourished.

I didn't know it at the time, but in retrospect it makes sense to me. Joesh, who's now a teenager, hates soft or mushy foods. He avoids anything creamy, and that includes sauces and even soup. Of course, he couldn't tell me this when he was a baby, and without a full set of teeth there wasn't much he could eat that wasn't soft. So during the few months until his weight went back up, I relied on screen time to feed him. The high chair would often be parked in the family room, right in front of the TV. I was desperate, tired, pregnant with my second child, and didn't know any better. Or maybe I did know better and chose not to think about it.

We parents might not realize the impact that screens are having on our children. That's why we need the science and research to help inform our decision making. Sometimes we use tech as a crutch because we want our lives to be easier, and in some cases tech can save us in the moment. So while we shouldn't shame people for handing their child an iPad from time to time, we still need to remember that sometimes the things that make your life easier in the short term can actually make it much more challenging and messy over the long term. Although feeding Joesh in front of the TV helped in the moment, it could have set him up for a habit of mindless, distracted eating. And once those habits are developed, mindlessness and distraction can spill over into other areas of life, like doing homework or having conversations.

I can't turn back the clock, but I can evaluate my behaviours and learn from the past. What we can all do is support our fellow parents, educators, and everyone else who interacts with children—by offering up ideas, strategies, and a helping hand. We must build that community of support, since we all want the same thing for all children: for each and every one of them to reach their own unique and full potential.

"OUR LIVES ARE BUT A MASS OF HABITS"

The 150 times your kids unlocked their phones yesterday weren't the result of 150 well-reasoned decisions. They were born of habits—urges that most of us barely recognize or understand.

Our habits are actions and behaviours we perform subconsciously. Every experience, thought, and feeling triggers thousands of neurons that in turn form a neural trail in our brains. I like to think of them as trails through a forest that develop through repetitive use. Over time, as we repeat behaviours, those neural trails become well-worn and easier to navigate; messages telling us to enact those behaviours begin to transmit faster and faster. With enough repetition, they become automatic.

New habits are hard to activate because they're just narrow trails amid a jungle of neurons. That's also why unknown trails can feel dangerous or exhausting, pushing us to stick to familiar trails.

Think back to when you were first learning to tie your shoelaces. At first it was a struggle, requiring all your attention. But with enough practice your brain eventually started shifting into autopilot whenever you pulled on your shoes. Even tasks that seem impossibly complex at first, like learning how to play the piano, speak French, or operate a new TV remote, become second nature after we perform them many times. (Well, not the remote—I have a feeling I'll always have to rely on my kids for that.)

There's a reason for this. Our brains are constantly looking for shortcuts. By mindlessly executing complex tasks, they're able to stop working so hard and divert focus to other, more pressing work. After all, if you had to concentrate every time you brushed your teeth or made a pot of coffee, you'd never have time to think about anything else!

From the moment we wake up to the moment we go to bed, our minds are largely on autopilot. According to a 2006 study by Duke University researchers, more than 40 percent of our daily activities are actually habits. Pioneering psychologist William James was righter than he knew when he wrote in 1892 that "all our life, so far as it has a definite form, is but a mass of habits."

CHANGE IS POSSIBLE

It's true that trails travelled for years become stronger, and the behaviours associated with them are often automatic. This is known as the Hebbian law; it tells us that "neurons that fire together wire together." And it often means that the older we get, the harder it becomes to change our habits. Forming a new habit when you're sixty can be like trying to slash your way through a dense jungle. But the good news is that your children's brains—and their innate human potential—are far more plastic and amenable to change than you might realize. The brain can form fresh neural pathways. Habits can be altered, ignored, replaced. And young children have more open space for new trails in their cortex, meaning they're more neuroplastic and able to change.

Still, we can't simply impose good habits onto our kids. If they feel forced to do something, they're going to wire a negative association with that habit. According to a 2018 study by Iowa State University researchers, how we feel about exercise as adults may even be rooted in our childhood experiences of gym class! These researchers found that unpleasant memories of P.E. correlated with a lingering resistance to exercise, even decades later. Participants who loved gym class and recalled positive experiences, on the other hand, were more likely to report that they found exercise enjoyable and tended to be active.

Similarly, if you force your daughter to practise the cello for ninety minutes as soon as she gets home from school every day—when she's feeling tired, hungry, and cranky—odds are she's not going to wire a deep love for the cello. I see this all the time in youth sports. A kid takes a liking to soccer and shows a natural talent for it. Her parents start pushing her, forcing her into camps, repetitive drills, tryouts for elite teams. In doing so, they can end up quashing that child's love and passion for the game. We need to remember that lasting good habits have to be intrinsic—they need to come from within. And we can ruin natural passion, talent, and perfectly good habits by wiring negative associations to them.

The opposite is also true. Think of a class you didn't like in school that suddenly became exciting once you had a teacher who brought a lot of energy and passion to the classroom. So by collaborating with our children and wiring a new habit with fun, humour, and positivity, odds are they're going to associate good feelings with it.

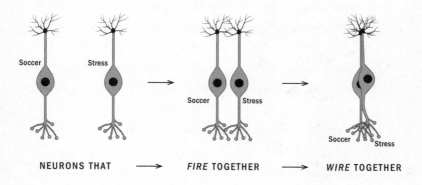

NEURONS THAT ⟶ *FIRE* TOGETHER ⟶ *WIRE* TOGETHER

"BAD" HABITS

Of course there's a dark side to habits, namely that our kids can also pick up bad ones like, say, perfectionism, impatience, overeating, multitasking, or procrastination. And once a habit emerges, those neural patterns are worn into our memory bank, the brain region called the hippocampus. Once encoded there, they may never truly disappear. To this day, whenever I see Joesh mindlessly eating in front of the TV, I wonder how much of that is choice or automatic programming from the months he ate while watching *Finding Nemo*. Luckily, though, we mostly eat at the table, so he was able to build new pathways that are taking over. Unless we help children rewire new habits, old patterns will unfold automatically. Even years after quitting, smokers, for example, still occasionally feel the urge to light up when they crack a cold beer or get into the car after work, whatever their old trigger used to be.

And today's gadgets have the power to reinforce some pretty awful habits—being glued to your phone, not looking at people, sitting with bad posture, not moving, staying indoors, checking your phone at night, in the bathroom, during dinner . . . the list goes on.

Indeed, our kids are now using their phones so much that they're being diagnosed with repetitive stress injuries: "texting thumb," "text neck," and "cellphone elbow" among them. Phones are also impairing our kids' ability to remember. They're making it harder for them to daydream and think creatively. They're impacting their ability to make friends and learn social etiquette. They're making them more vulnerable to anxiety, depression, and loneliness.

If your son reaches for his phone to make him feel better whenever he's angry or anxious, he's wiring an unhealthy coping mechanism with these emotions. Instead of learning how to deal with them—an important part of growing up—he's learning to check out, to avoid feeling difficult feelings. He's not learning how to self-regulate, cope with life, or solve problems. This means that whenever he's sad or angry, he's likely to reach for a screen. These feelings can become exacerbated in a feedback loop. That is, your son may go online to escape what's happening in the real world, and then being online causes him to feel his peers are accomplishing more, doing more, and connecting more than he is. This leads to his feeling even worse about himself and thus trying to escape even further.

HEALTHY HABITS START WITH YOU

Your son may continue that pattern into university and the workplace. As life gets more real, he may turn to other distractions like overwork, overspending, overeating, pornography, alcohol, or drugs to help him check out.

A big part of growing up is acquiring a set of skills to help navigate school, work, relationships. These skills include learning to communicate, to resolve conflict, to build friendships and romantic relationships. But if your kids are only ever navigating friendships and breaking up with romantic partners on their phones, they won't have a framework or practice for how to do this in the real world. If the age of connectedness has taught us anything, it's that being connected to everyone all the time is actually making us less attentive to the social skills that are most important for future success.

Habits established in childhood are the foundation for future behaviours, so take advantage of your child's formative years. Guide them towards the most important habits early and help them maintain them as they mature. Don't put this off until you think your kids can truly understand what you're talking about. They're picking up a lot more than you realize. And remember, the human brain is neuroplastic—so it's never too late to build or change habits.

Just to be clear, we can't do this work *for* our children. We can't control their every moment. But nor we can absent ourselves in the belief that positive behaviours and habits will simply emerge on their own. Children are *relational learners*. Their experiences and the feelings they have for their parents and teachers matter. As parents, then, we're most effective when we stand shoulder to shoulder with our children, providing love, inspiration, support, and guidance through life's ups and downs.

There are many approaches to parenting, but below I present the three commonly referenced styles. As you read their descriptions, consider where your current approach tends to fit, and what style of parenting seems best for fostering confident, self-motivated children.

Authoritarian parents believe they absolutely know best. This is a style that has high expectations for external performance and image (awards, grades, appearance) but little focus on the internal qualities of kindness, community mindedness, and self-motivation. There are two types of authoritarian parenting styles. *Authoritarian-directing* parents, so-called "tiger" or "shark" parents, set and push rules and expectations; they say what goes and leave little room for autonomy. *Authoritarian-protecting* parents, or "helicopter parents," tend to hover, micromanage, and rescue their children when things go wrong. Children of authoritarian parents have higher rates of anxiety, depression, and perfectionism and a lower ability to adapt to change, overcome failure, and demonstrate resilience.

Permissive parents are at the other end of the spectrum. They're no less imbalanced than authoritarian parents. I refer to them as "jellyfish parents" because they tend to be spineless and aimless in their approach. This type of parent doesn't offer their child much in the way of rules, guidance, direction, and focus. Children of permissive parents lack internal values, have poor impulse control, look to peers and media for guidance, and are more likely to develop problems with authority figures and substances.

Authoritative parents are a balance between the two extremes of authoritarian and permissive parents. They have clear expectations for their children and are collaborative in decision making. They're known as "dolphin parents" and, like the body of the marine animal, they're firm and flexible: firm on internal values and character yet flexible with the child's interests, choices, and self-expression. They value play, community, and a healthy, balanced lifestyle. Children of authoritative parents exhibit better mental health, problem solving, impulse control, academic performance, social consciousness, adaptability, and self-motivation than the other two styles.

To me, results matter, and thus I believe that authoritative parenting is the most effective parenting style. In fact I developed an entire framework around it in a book, titled *The Dolphin Parent: A Guide to Raising Healthy, Happy, and Self-Motivated Kids*.

Dolphin parenting is about guiding rather than directing, and encouraging rather than instructing. Dolphin parents teach their children by modelling good behaviour. My favourite example of this style is drawn from nature. When a dolphin calf is born its mother gently nudges her calf along to the surface of the ocean, where it can take its first breath. Rather than lifting her young to the surface, she models swimming for it. For the first several months the dolphin mom guides, models, and instructs when needed, all while staying close to her calf, rarely leaving its side.

Dolphin parenting is so effective because it emphasizes the importance of a balanced lifestyle, focusing on self-care, play, exploration, social bonding, and contribution. This is why I consider the terms *dolphin parenting*, *balanced parenting*, and *intuitive parenting* to be interchangeable. The goals are the same: nurturing curious, confident, connected, adaptable, and resilient kids through the dolphin parenting behaviours of bonding, role modelling, and guiding.

KEY DOLPHIN PARENT BEHAVIOURS

Bonding: Being bonded means really knowing your child for who they are, not who you want them to be. It's about accepting your child despite what you may see, loving her, and connecting with her not just as your child, but as an individual.

Role modelling: Acting as a role model demonstrates to your child that what you do and how you exist in the world reflects who you are internally. Role modelling means using your genuine self to teach life lessons. Children are, of course, also *observational learners*. Every day we're modelling behaviours for them. For example, if we have a phone permanently in hand we're effectively saying "This is acceptable." For some children, that message will be louder and clearer than whatever you may be telling them while you hold the phone. Role modelling is about showing who you are on the inside through what you do on the outside. Children know when a mismatch exists between the two, so don't even bother preaching something you don't really believe.

Guiding: Nurture your child from a place of knowledge and authority while also respecting their autonomy. Parents who guide give their kids a tour of the world, pointing out life's ups and downs while providing support along the way. They say things like "Hey, life can be unfair," "These are the ways people resolve conflict," and "This is a beautiful moment to celebrate." Guiding doesn't mean pushing, hovering, micromanaging, or forcing; it means accepting that your child's journey belongs to them.

Although it would be ideal if we could all be perfect role models guiding our children in perfectly bonded bliss all the time, it's just not a reality! I remember once pulling out my phone while my kids and I waited in a shopping mall parking lot. They called me out, saying I was a "hypocrite." I had to explain that I wasn't playing video games or scrolling social media, I was paying bills online. I also told them that I often book our vacations, register them in activities, reply to patient emails, read neuroscience articles, and write notes for my books—all on my phone. Of course, sometimes I *am* a hypocrite and check my phone during dinner. That certainly deserves to be called out!

Fostering key parenting behaviours as you read and implementing some of the suggestions in this book will ensure that you maintain a strong, positive relationship with your child. As we grapple with today's pervasive digital culture, it's up to us to help our children understand both the wonder and the risk of tech and to establish healthy, constructive tech habits. For kids, the tech world is their native environment just as much as the physical world is. They need us to exist in that space with them in the same way they need us in their offline worlds.

And our kids aren't just passively consuming tech. They're active participants, too: creators, collaborators, even influencers. Some are uploading unboxing toy reviews and "Watch Me Play Overwatch" or "How to Draw Minecraft Characters" videos to their YouTube channels. They're posting their glittery, pastel-coloured #DIYslime videos to Instagram or participating in global activism from their bedrooms. Some even earn big audiences and serious money for this. Many are simply exploring new passions and interests and learning to communicate across mediums, an increasingly necessary skill. Like it or not, then, this is all part of modern parenting.

EDUCATING FUTURE-READY KIDS

Compared to the world our children are entering, previous generations had it easy. They had to get an education, then find a job. But the decent-wage, low- and middle-skilled jobs that sustained the middle class throughout the last century are rapidly disappearing. That trend is irreversible, and widening inequality, a parallel trend, is rising in step. Our children will enter the workforce at a time of unparalleled economic, social, and technological change, with disruptive shifts in jobs and skills already impacting every industry. Rapid technological developments in artificial intelligence (A.I.), machine learning, and automation are also underway. According to a 2018 McKinsey Global Institute report, one-third of American workers may have to switch jobs in the next fifteen years because of A.I.

And information has never been anywhere near as accessible as it is now. In the past it was those who acquired the most knowledge who tended to be the most valued. Rote memorization was key to a student's success. But thanks to technology, it's no longer essential to memorize multiplication tables, chemical formulas, and world capitals. Students no longer need to know the right answer to a given question; they can just Google it. Today, it's far more important to know how to ask the right questions and to foster the crucial skills that can't be co-opted by computers— skills that will help students succeed in today's highly social, ultra-competitive, tech-based economy.

We can think of these skills as the new future-ready intelligence of the Consciousness Quotient (CQ)—a term I coined in *The Dolphin Parent*. Unlike the "left brain" Intelligence Quotient (IQ) and "right brain" Emotional Quotient (EQ), CQ elicits our whole human intelligence system. And the good news is that these CQ skills are available in us all, developed as they are through our neuroplastic trails.

THE FIVE CQ SKILLS:
- **Creativity** means thinking *beyond* traditional ideas, rules, patterns, and relationships. It means generating new, original ideas.
- **Critical thinking** includes open-minded analysis, interpretation, explanation, and problem-solving. Knowing how to ask the right question is more important than knowing the right answer.
- **Communication** means being able to express yourself across different media—from essays and emails to infographics, social media posts, messaging apps, and digital communities.

- **Collaboration** means learning from, inspiring, and working in tandem with others from diverse and global backgrounds.
- **Contribution** means bringing value to your team and making the world a better place in small or big ways.

The five elements of CQ will help your children thrive through some of the biggest changes in human history. Age-old systems are being disrupted. Innovations in education, transportation, communication, and banking are occurring at breakneck speed. That's why it's so important not to fear technology—and why I'll also explore the healthy ways in which our children can embrace tech and use it to thrive.

TRY YOUR BEST

As parents, it's important to remember that we can only ever try our best. Although I am blessed in many ways, I'm a person with three kids, two of whom have significant learning differences; I have a serious medical condition and a career that's always changing. I'm fortunate to have a supportive husband, but he too is stretched in countless ways. We've got bills to pay, aging bodies, aging parents, basketball practices, and gymnastics camps. We get tired. Sometimes on the weekend, we let our kids veg out in front of the TV for a couple of hours, and they're doing just fine. Further, I think tech can be incredibly beneficial to kids. For example, certain video games can be a great way for them to bond with one another. When my sons play *FIFA* or *NBA Live*, they're laughing with and catcalling their cousins in the U.K. and the U.S. These are relationships I don't think would have developed if not for video games. So for those moments of connection, and many others like it, my family's digital devices deserve our gratitude.

The point is to teach your kids to use tech wisely, to not allow it to use them and consume their lives. Like everything else in life, we are what we repeatedly do. If you want to be good at math or soccer, you must practise math or soccer. Thus, we must make sure technology doesn't impede our kids' chances to practise real life. We must also help them practise using tech in an empowering way. We have to help them fully and deeply understand technology's incredible benefits as well as its serious drawbacks so that they can master the fire of our time.

REMEMBER . . .

- Our habits, or neural trails, are like trails in a forest—over time, messages that travel the same neural trail begin to transmit faster and faster. With enough repetition, they become automatic.
- Our habits are actions and behaviours wired subconsciously through these trails.
- Neurons that fire together wire together—emotions and associations become embedded into our habits.
- Habits established in childhood are the foundation for future behaviours.
- Our children's brains—and their innate human potential—are far more plastic and amenable to change, positivity, and inspiration than we may realize.
- The brain can form fresh neural pathways: habits can be changed, ignored, and replaced.
- The work of creating new habits takes focus, motivation, effort, and time. And the older children get, the harder this becomes.
- The authoritative, collaborative dolphin relationship can help guide children onto positive trails and rewire negative ones.
- The guiding dolphin interpersonal style also leads to future-ready children who have the positive mindset and life skills to navigate our rapidly changing world.
- The new twenty-first-century intelligence is the Consciousness Quotient (CQ), comprising communication, collaboration, critical thinking, creativity, and contribution.

SOLUTIONS

The Solutions sections in this book are made up of practical advice for tackling specific tech-related problems you might face. The suggestions here are meant to be combined in a way that best suits your needs and those of the children in your life.

So far we've discussed why technology has been designed to manipulate our attention and how this impacts the developing brain. We've also learned about the power of habits—how they become wired with our emotions via neuroplastic trails. As parents, our role is to guide children towards habits that serve them and away from habits that will harm them. The best way to do this is to embrace an authoritative dolphin parenting style and guide your child towards the twenty-first-century intelligence of CQ.

In the pages that follow you'll find suggestions for helping your child establish positive habits for life. I'll also set the stage for how to best introduce technology to your child and what early habits will help them optimize its benefits while minimizing its drawbacks.

KEY STRATEGIES

DON'T

- Assume a product is healthy just because it's available
- Think anyone else is looking out for your child's best interest
- Expect someone else to solve the problems associated with your kids' tech use
- Let children use tech without a clear purpose, limits, and monitoring
- Use tech as a toy

DO

- Delay the introduction of tech for as long as possible
- Use tech as a tool to accomplish something
- Remember that initially tech time shouldn't be alone time
- Set clear house rules for tech use

ESTABLISH HEALTHY LIFE HABITS EARLY

Neuroplasticity is the ability of the brain to evolve and change over the course of an individual's life. You now know that the brains of young children and teens are highly neuroplastic. That means that it's much easier to establish healthy habits and change negative ones prior to the age of twenty-five than it is after.

Below I've outlined five essential ingredients that promote neuroplasticity and healthy life habits in your children. I'm the first to admit that, although these elements may be simple, it's not always easy to implement them. For instance, I'm intimately familiar with the science of sleep, but that doesn't always mean I'm getting enough of it!

Make Sleep a Priority

While we sleep, our brains file important information from our day-to-day lives, which supports learning and memory, and discard what isn't needed.

The American Academy of Sleep Medicine recommends that every night . . .

- Infants aged four to twelve months sleep twelve to sixteen hours.
- Children aged one to two sleep eleven to fourteen hours.
- Children aged three to five sleep ten to thirteen hours.
- Children aged six to twelve sleep nine to twelve hours.
- Teenagers aged thirteen to eighteen sleep eight to ten hours.
- Adults should sleep seven to nine hours.

Make Sure Your Kids Are Well-Nourished and Hydrated

Our brains are over 70 percent water. When we're even mildly dehydrated, our functioning can become impaired.

Optimal brain health requires a healthy variety of foods. A diverse diet of generally non-processed whole foods is a good rule of thumb. And since the majority of the brain tissue is fat, we need to make sure our children eat healthy fats, like omega-3 fatty acids from fish, nuts, and avocados, for example. However, given today's food wars and what I believe to be an unhealthy obsession with "eating right," it's important to remember that eating should never be stressful. If it is, your child's body—and yours!—will start releasing stress hormones, which will counteract the benefits of healthy eating.

It's critically important, meanwhile, to minimize substances that negatively impact brain health; these include aspartame and processed sugar.

Kids Need Cardio

Cardiovascular exercise is any activity that will get your kids' hearts and lungs going, like running, hiking, or biking. Your kids are in the beneficial "cardio zone" when their heart rate goes up, they feel short of breath, and they can't hold a conversation. Doing this improves blood flow to the brain and increases oxygen levels, which in turn increases neuron growth. Children and teens age six and older need at least one hour of physical activity per day, and most of that hour should be spent doing either moderate or vigorous cardiovascular exercise. Children also need to engage in muscle-strengthening and bone-strengthening activities such as climbing stairs, jumping, hopping, skipping, and dancing at least three days per week. The bottom line is that an active body leads to a stronger mind for learning. And if your child develops a habit of being active when they're young, they're more likely to be active into adulthood.

Let Them Play!

All mammals learn by playing, whether they're chimpanzees, puppies, or children. In learning through play—which is essentially having fun with trial and error—children figure out what works best for them, and they become comfortable with uncertainty. Ideally, play should be unstructured, allowing children to experiment without judgment or evaluation. This makes learning safe and fun. So parents, try not to analyze every soccer move, comment on their storytelling details, or evaluate their artwork!

Don't Forget: Love Powers the Mind

Kids learn best in safe, supportive, loving relationships. Feeling connected and safe reduces stress, while feeling alone or fearful increases it. Remember, though, that love doesn't mean letting them do whatever they want whenever they want—that's jellyfish parenting. They need dolphin love that's unconditional but paired with clear limits and rules around behaviour. That's when kids feel connected and safe. Feeling love, positivity, and optimism engenders the growth of more connective neural fibres in their brains. These fibres play a key role in increasing cognitive function, so if you want your child to be smart, happy, and strong, love them for exactly who they are!

ESTABLISH HEALTHY TECH HABITS FOR YOUR CHILD

Now that you know how to create healthy habits in general, let's set the foundation for healthy tech habits in the home.

Delay, Delay, Delay

The first thing you can do for your children is delay the introduction of screen time for as long as possible, allowing them the space they need to first develop important life skills and habits. This will set the course for long-term health, happiness, self-motivation, and success.

If the skills below aren't somewhat mastered before introducing tech, your child is at risk of associating them only with their technology usage, and troubles can follow. For example, if children learn to bond with friends through a device, they've "wired and fired" these skills dependent on technology and may not feel comfortable or able to do it in real life. So they need to be encouraged to develop healthy friendships and bonds in real life (IRL) long before they do it online. Similarly, if they're introduced to video games before they've learned to manage their time or regulate their emotions, they're more likely to become out of control with gaming or use it to mask or avoid their emotions.

Please encourage the building, mastering, and maintaining of three key life skills—emotional regulation, social skills, and time management—before and while you introduce technology to your children. If you can honestly answer yes to the following three questions, it may be the right time to introduce your child to a new technology.

1. **Emotional regulation:** Are they able to feel and regulate their emotions?

2. **Social skills:** Are they able to interact and communicate face to face with others in a collaborative and confident way?

3. **Time management:** Are they able to move on from something fun and maintain an awareness of their time commitments for daily tasks such as sleep, movement, or learning?

How to Schedule Tech Time

The most common question I receive from parents is "How much screen time is okay for my child?" I wish I could provide a specific answer, but the truth is, every child, every family, and every situation is different. When it comes to tech, we must be firm about preventing harm and be flexible with daily life. These are my guidelines:

- Screen time for children younger than two isn't recommended at all.
- For children aged two to five, screen time should be limited to less than one hour per day. But remember, it's best to delay tech time as long as possible, so if you can avoid it at this stage, that's still best.

For all other age groups, schedule purposeful tech use around life activities instead of scheduling life around tech. This will set kids up to prioritize real-life activities as they get older and to understand the role tech should play in their day-to-day lives:

1. Take a sheet of lined paper.
2. Block off twenty-four lines. These will represent the twenty-four hours in a day.
3. Block off the hours needed for sleep, hygiene, eating, chores, exercise, relationships, school, homework (may require tech), and non-tech play. You may also need time for other important activities your family may value, such as going to church/temple, service work, and caring for pets.
4. The time left over can be *part* of their tech time, but it doesn't have to be.

Tech Time Shouldn't Be Alone Time
To build positive, lasting tech-use habits for the future,

encourage your kids to spend their tech time in the living room or kitchen, not their bedrooms. Take a collaborative, curious, and connecting approach to learning about tech use and misuse. What I mean is that you should try to learn more about your kids through their tech use and use it in turn to teach important life lessons. Try to identify their interests, passions, and concerns, and talk with each other about any issues or problems that might come up.

Here are a few tips:

- Be present and engaged when screens are in use. Whenever possible, co-view with children.
- Have conversations! Ask questions about your kids' favourite games, shows, apps, and characters. Discuss ideas and issues they learn about through a TV show or a game. This is an opportunity for bonding, learning from your child, and teaching your child.
- Help kids recognize and question stereotyping, advertising messages, and other problematic content. Ask them what they think of such issues.

Set the Expectation of Limits, Independence, and Fun
Just as you can't be with your child 24/7, nor should you obsess over their technology use. It is best to get into the habit of checking in, asking questions, and monitoring their use. When done early in life, your child will understand that this is part of your role as a parent and there'll be less resistance later. You can also lay the groundwork for conveying your expectation and trust that they'll start making healthy choices:

- Encourage independent analysis and decision making when possible. For example, if your child wants to watch a movie or buy a new video game, have them check the ratings and explain why it's a good choice for them. If they can't read yet, have them verbally explain or draw a picture.
- If your child wants more time online, ask them how they plan to manage their time and self-regulate their use.
- Check in by asking your child to print out and report their browser history, then discuss what they're seeing.
- Discuss content and prioritize educational, age-appropriate, high-quality, interactive programming. Work together to set up software for filters or for restricting access to inappropriate content. For example, use Kiddle instead of Google (when my son was into snakes and Googled "anaconda," he ended up on a porn site!).

Model Healthy Habits

We've all heard it a million times because it's true: kids learn more from what we do than what we say. So there's little point in providing instructions for something you're not practising yourself.

- Show your child that you make it a habit to choose healthy alternatives to tech time, such as reading, outdoor play, and creative, hands-on activities.
- When you're on your device, explain how you're using it as a tool and communicate your purpose. I often say to my kids something like "I have to use my phone now to pay bills/send a message to Grandma/look up research for my book. I'm not scrolling social media or playing video games!"

- When using a screen, role-model putting it away or looking away from it, maintaining eye contact, and sustaining your attention when communicating.
- Model presence by *not* responding to a ringer, notification, or message in front of children. Say things like "I'll check that later since we're having a conversation now. I'm going to shut off my phone so I don't keep getting interrupted."
- Develop a family plan for your tech use by setting SMART goals (pages 254–55). You may even want to include when, how, and where screens may (and may not) be≈used in your home.

3

HOOKED: Dopamine and How to Manage Technology's Addictive Power

How use doth breed a habit in man!

—WILLIAM SHAKESPEARE,

THE TWO GENTLEMEN OF VERONA,

ACT 5, SCENE 4

IN MY PRACTICE I'm increasingly seeing beautiful, intelligent, kind-hearted children and teens, full of potential, who are losing control of their minds and lives to screens. Many of them are spending countless hours staring into a glowing monitor on some days, neglecting their schoolwork, their families, and themselves as they scroll social media or listen on a headset to strangers discussing strategy for *World of Warcraft*. They're no different from people I've treated with addictions to cocaine or alcohol. Their lives are ruined. Their interpersonal relationships are nonexistent. They're in terrible physical shape.

To help you understand how technology can take over a young person's life, I want to tell you a true story about a young man named Kyle. He was raised in a loving, middle-class home in a small town in the United States. His dad is a molecular biologist.

His mom, Michelle, was once a retail manager and now advocates for special-needs kids in schools.

Throughout high school, Kyle was a high achiever. He was valedictorian and the top student of his graduating class. He was also a three-sport student athlete, a student council member, and a trumpet player in the honours band. He didn't smoke, use drugs, or drink alcohol. He was afraid they might somehow impact his future prospects, he once told me. But when he got to university, Kyle began feeling overwhelmed by the competitive environment. The stress he'd faced as a grade 12 student in high school deepened. Video games, which he'd been playing since he was six and used to cope with stress, became his only escape. He started playing late into the night. Soon he was skipping class, unable to put down his controller. Before long, gaming took over his life. He was forced to drop out of school and move back home. When his parents tried barring him from gaming he'd jump mediums, obsessively scrolling through websites, news sites, social media.

When Kyle couldn't get onto a screen, "it was abject anxiety, sadness and rage," Michelle explains. Her "easy-peasy kid who was so patient and kind" would turn into a "mean and inconsolable tyrant." Kyle hated himself for it. He vacillated between being remorseful for his treatment of his mom to hating her for getting between him and his video games.

By then Kyle was fighting with his parents every day—screaming at them and banging his head on the table, doing anything he could just to avoid talking to them about his gaming. Using consumed him, he says. "I lived to use and used to live. I was utterly broken and at the mercy of my addiction." Counselling wasn't working. Kyle had his therapists convinced that he had a handle on his "passion," and they just thought he needed to grow up.

But addiction runs through Michelle's family. She understood that her son had become a full-blown gaming addict. Finally, she took action. She gave Kyle an ultimatum: go to recovery or she'd leave to go live with her sister. Michelle could no longer handle his rage, his depression, the dark cloud that seemed to hang over their family.

THE ADDICTIVE POWER OF GAMING

Whenever Kyle made a kill or levelled up in a game he'd be hit with a rush from the release of dopamine, which works by filling us with a sense of pleasure and excitement. And because we like feeling pleasure, our brains instinctively remember what caused us to feel that way. So the small hits of dopamine just made Kyle crave more—more games, more dopamine, more bursts of pleasure. For a while it felt as though all he was doing was chasing "dopamine hits," he says. In between, though, he felt dead inside.

In 2018 the WHO added "gaming disorder" to its International Classification of Diseases, defining it as an excessive preoccupation with video games resulting in significant academic, social, or occupational impairment for at least twelve months.

Kyle knew he was depressed. He was flunking out of school; he had few friends and was living in his parents' basement. But when he was gaming, he felt talented. He had friends. He could escape to a world where he was the hero. In recovery, he came to understand that video games were filling primal needs and desires that were going unmet. That's why they became so addictive. That's why he was having so much trouble giving them up.

WHAT GAMING GAVE KYLE

Positive reinforcement: By accumulating rewards—finding a clue, getting a high score, levelling up—Kyle felt he was growing increasingly competent. As he began struggling in other areas of his life, the sense of accomplishment that came with those rewards was intoxicating.

Companionship: During the first gaming boom in the 1980s, most video games were single player. Massively multiplayer online games, known as MMOs, the type Kyle preferred, allowed him to play in large groups. This fed his need for connection. Logging off was hard for Kyle, who became bonded to his teammates. IRL, he'd lost touch with his old pals. He was embarrassed about what had become of him. Online, no one knew of his failures.

A new reality: The shoddy graphics of *Super Mario Bros.* are a thing of the past. Kyle was immersing himself in exquisitely detailed, constantly shifting, often beautiful virtual realms. The real world seemed dull by comparison.

The chance to be a hero: Some games allowed Kyle to create his own character and then embark on a unique adventure.

CHASING THE NEXT DOPAMINE HIT

Dopamine is playing a role not only in video games but in most of the media we now consume. Facebook's founding president, Sean Parker, who began running the blockbuster social network in 2004 when it was just five months old, now acknowledges that the platform was built on a neurochemical. Dopamine, Parker says, is the secret sauce powering Facebook's success.

The thinking, Parker explained in a 2017 interview, was "How do we consume as much of your time and conscious attention as possible?" Facebook recognized that it needed "to give you a little dopamine hit every once in a while, because someone liked or commented on a photo or a post." Doing that would prompt users to share more content, which would bring more likes and comments. "It's a social-validation feedback loop," Parker said, "exactly the kind of thing that a hacker like myself would come up with, because you're exploiting a vulnerability in human psychology."

As Parker, who's since left the company, pointed out, once our brains begin associating social media with a reward, we're going to want to keep refreshing our feeds to get the next dopamine hit.

Think back to the time you posted a photo of your newborn or a flattering picture of yourself on social media. Remember the rush of happiness you felt seeing dozens of supportive messages? That feeling came from dopamine. Released to reward us for doing something that keeps us alive, like hunting, gathering, or bonding, it forms the basis of our brain's positive feedback loop, a primal system as old as life itself.

The process is key to our survival. It motivates us to seek out food or shelter or to turn up the heat. But if it becomes dysregulated, it can also cause cravings—for the exquisite ping of social affirmation that comes when people retweet or "like" something we've written. It makes us feel happy and loved. But in many cases, it can become tied to our self-worth as individuals.

At this point it must be becoming clear how this can lead to addiction. While our stomachs will send a signal to our brains telling us to stop eating when we're full, social media apps are deliberately designed to override internal cues through more offers of dopamine hits. Even when we're aware that our scrolling is making us feel angry, anxious, or depressed, our brains keep telling us to go back, to refresh our feeds, to keep scrolling.

In a famous 1950s psychological experiment, two McGill University neuroscientists, Peter Milner and James Olds, implanted small electrodes in the brains of rats. They placed them in the *nucleus accumbens*, the area of the brain that regulates dopamine production—and that lights up when a drug addict ingests fentanyl or a gambler hits the jackpot. Olds and Milner labelled it the "pleasure centre."

The scientists also placed a lever inside the rats' cages. Every time a rat pushed on the lever it would stimulate the electrode in the animal's pleasure centre. Left alone, the rats kept pressing their levers. Again and again—as many as seven thousand times a day. Even when they were thirsty they went for the lever, not water. They ignored their hunger. They refused sex. All they wanted to do was keep hitting that lever.

Does their behaviour remind you of anything? Think back to Kyle, who was staying up all night, skipping school to play video games. He stopped exercising and eating healthily. All Kyle wanted to do was hit that lever of his own. Maybe you've witnessed similar behaviour in a young person you know—a teenager who keeps scrolling social media into the wee hours, a young person so fixated on their phone that they ignore the people around them? In 2017, a seventeen-year-old boy from Guangzhou suffered a stroke and nearly died after playing *Honour of Kings*, the hit Chinese fantasy role-playing game, for forty hours straight. And the Japanese government estimates that there are 1.15 million *hikikomori*, young people who've withdrawn from society and are staying in their homes or bedrooms for months and even years on end playing video games and surfing the web. They rely instead on their parents and families to take care of them.

There's a big difference between tech tools designed to help people improve their lives and those designed to hook people on their products. The way I see it, tech that kids are actively using in the service of their goals is positive tech. Tech that they're passively consuming, on the other hand, is negative. These companies are using kids in the service of their own goals.

WHY TECHNOLOGY IS DESIGNED FOR ADDICTION

In most cases, apps and social networks aren't charging for access. The internet is sustained by clicks and eyeballs. For big tech, the goal, as Parker explained, is getting users to spend as much time as possible on their sites. This, in Silicon Valley's sanitized vernacular, is what's known as "user engagement." After all, the longer Twitter, Facebook, and YouTube can keep us "engaged" on their sites, the more they can charge advertisers.

To maintain revenue growth, social networks and apps are constantly searching for new ways to fight your brain—to stop you from logging off or deleting their apps and engaging in real-life activities. At their disposal are hundreds of years of publicly funded research from neuroscience, psychology, linguistics, cognitive science, and social behaviour.

But what few children (and parents) understand is that when an online service is free, they're not the customer, they're the product. Corporations like Google, Facebook, Instagram, and Amazon, whose sites you've visited, then closely track your likes, purchases, and location, information they can package and sell to advertisers. This puts tech executives in a bind, says Bill Davidow, a former vice-president of Intel Corp. "Either they hijack neuroscience to gain market share and make large profits, or they let competitors do that and run away with the market."

Nowhere is the widespread desire for cracking the neurological code Facebook unravelled early on more brazen than at the controversial California start-up Dopamine Labs, which seeks to "surprise and hook" users by infusing apps and platforms with the same addictive powers as Instagram and Twitter. Dopamine Labs is the brainchild of two close friends, T. Dalton Combs, a neuro-economist, and Ramsay Brown, a neuropsychologist. "Since we've figured to some extent how these pieces of the brain that handle addiction are working, people have figured out how to juice them further and how to bake that information into apps," says Brown. He acknowledges that this power is both thrilling *and* terrifying: "We have the ability to twiddle some knobs in a machine-learning dashboard we build, and around the world hundreds of thousands of people are going to quietly change their behaviour in ways that, unbeknownst to them, feel second nature but are really by design."

What Brown is saying is that what might feel like conscious decisions are in reality hijacking methods that engineers are using to alter our behaviour.

SEVEN WAYS DEVELOPERS ARE MANIPULATING YOUR KIDS' MINDS

Developers like Sean Parker and neuropsychologists like Ramsay Brown understand precisely what causes dopamine surges in our brains and infuse their products with techniques that trigger their release. The most successful ones hook us by exploiting primal human needs: our need to be loved, connected, and recognized, to feel competent, to give and receive attention, to achieve something. Some argue that it's our job as parents to protect our kids from manipulative tactics like these. But we can't protect our kids and teens from something we don't even recognize ourselves.

So here are the common methods programmers use to capture your kids' attention. Once you become aware of them you can teach your children to spot them and understand them. This will help kids take back some control in their interactions with technology.

1. Red Alert!

We all know what red means: *Emergency! Urgent!* Red is the most intense and dynamic colour. In fact, it's known as a "trigger" colour: research shows that it can elevate your heart rate and blood pressure. It has also been shown to make people click at a higher rate than any other colour.

Originally, Facebook notifications were in blue. This was in keeping with the corporate brand, whose blue hue was famously selected because it's the one that founder Mark Zuckerberg, who is red-green colour-blind, can best see. But Facebook found that people tended to ignore these alerts. When they were changed to red, clicking suddenly went through the roof.

The industry took note. These days you'll find small red dots attached to apps all over your iPhone, begging you to open them. The next time you find yourself sitting with your kids, pull out your phone and show them these alerts that let you know a message is waiting for you or that someone has "liked" your status. Explain why they're red, and how we're biologically driven to want to open an app when we see red. You might want to show them how you can change your phone to greyscale so that everything appears in black and white, making it less stimulating, more boring, less appealing.

2. Social Approval

In the same way that we humans have a basic need for food and shelter, we also have an innate need to belong to a group and form deep relationships to others. Facebook "likes" and Instagram hearts play on this primal need for love and connection.

The world around us may have changed dramatically since paleolithic times, but our brains have not. On the savannah, we had to carefully manage our social standing within the tribe. Loners and cast-outs tended to get picked off. Your survival depended on being needed and appreciated.

During adolescence, we are acutely sensitive to social pressures and yearn to be included in the in-group. I find that many of my teen patients become obsessed with maintaining their social media presence, which is a way to affirm and display friendships, something we humans have been doing since time immemorial.

If you have a teenager in your life, you might consider telling them about the time you posted something to social media that didn't get any likes, and how it felt embarrassing and painful because it also felt like a public rejection. Let them know that while those painful feelings are real, the rejection was not. Facebook likes don't measure popularity. True friends love all of you—your flaws, your talents, your quirky sense of humour. Research shows your kids need one or two true friends, not eight hundred on social media.

You could also encourage them to use alternative platforms that don't track their users' data, don't display ads, and don't try to increase usage with likes and streaks.

3. Autoplay and Infinite Scroll

As YouTube and Netflix know, the easiest way to keep kids (and their parents!) from logging off is by autoplaying the next video by default. It's no surprise that binge watching suddenly spiked when Netflix first introduced the feature, which queues up the next episode after a ten-second countdown.

Social networking sites often exploit the same principle. By autofilling your feed and allowing you to scroll forever, these sites make it that much harder to log off.

The next time you're watching a series on Netflix with your child, hit pause when the next episode begins to autoplay. Explain why this happened. Remind them that they control how long they watch.

4. Variable Rewards

Counterintuitive though it may seem, the best way to keep young people checking Instagram is *not* by rewarding them every time they open the app. *Randomness* is what really gets them hooked. With comments and "likes" appearing on no set schedule, they're forced to keep compulsively checking the apps, never sure when they'll be rewarded with a hit of dopamine.

The scientific term for this is "variable rewards." And if you don't believe this works on humans, remember that this is the way slot machines—which account for some 80 percent of the average casino's revenues—are designed.

Tech engineers drew on the work of the American psychologist B.F. Skinner, who discovered the power of randomly doling out rewards in a series of experiments on pigeons. Skinner taught the pigeons to peck a button for food. But he learned he could drive the poor birds berserk by randomly rewarding them. They'd keep pecking and pecking, hoping to hit the jackpot. One kept pecking for food for sixteen hours straight!

Explain in simple terms to your teen that this is how social media works. Every time she opens Instagram, Snapchat, or Twitter she's effectively pulling on the arm of a slot machine. Will she be rewarded with a link to a fascinating story or a bunch of silly tweets? She doesn't know. That's what's driving her to keep refreshing her feed. Humans, like pigeons, crave predictability. Variability is our kryptonite. It drives us to do crazy things, like open Snapchat forty-five times in a single day.

Teach your kids to set aside a specific time every day to check social media for a clear purpose. For example, Joesh has friends in South Africa and Europe, and he's allowed to download Snapchat and Instagram only on Sunday afternoons to connect with them.

5. Novelty Bias

Novelty bias simply means that we humans love new things. We were hardwired this way. In the paleolithic era, the ability to recognize and respond to new, often dangerous, things was key to our survival.

These days, it's making us react helplessly to the buzz of incoming information. It's why social media apps are constantly nagging us to turn on their notifications. When an alert tells us that a WhatsApp message or a news story awaits us, we have a hard time ignoring it. My advice: teach your kids to turn off their notifications and avoid becoming subject to the randomness of them. It's another way to take back control from the apps and other platforms they're using.

6. Fear of Missing Out (FOMO)

FOMO, or the fear of missing out, is one of the main reasons we stay on social media even though we know, rationally, that it's an anxiety-inducing time suck. If we delete social media there's always the chance that we'll miss an invite, a sale, or a message from a friend. And for adolescents, who are already anxious about fitting in, not being in on a joke, or seeming uncool, the stakes can feel extraordinarily high.

As parents, it's our job to help our children understand that they won't miss what they don't see, and to let them know that the truly important messages will reach them whether or not they're on Instagram. And if they do actually miss out on something, that is ok too.

7. Social Reciprocity

We're wired to want to get back to others when they reach out. This is known as social reciprocity—the back-and-forth flow of social interaction that makes us want to respond to a positive action with another positive action.

When Facebook tells the sender that a recipient has read their message, it triggers our hardwired sense of social reciprocity. Snapchat and WhatsApp have taken this one step further: users are informed the *second* a friend begins typing a message to them. To a teen, the need to respond can feel overwhelming—more urgent than acknowledging their parents or letting out their bark-ing dog who desperately needs to pee. To our paleolithic brains, ignoring a Twitter DM or a friend request on Instagram can feel like a potentially dangerous social gaffe.

Tell your kids about the good old days when phones hung from walls and didn't join you for walks or in the bathroom. No one expected you to be home at all times to answer them. You got back to your friends when you could. That's still true today, even if methods of communication have sped up. Let your kids know that they don't need to instantly reply to messages. Help them make a habit of letting messages sit unopened for a day or more. Teach them the importance of thinking before they text, and to *never* send an email when they feel angry or upset.

LET'S GET REAL ABOUT OUR KIDS' WILLPOWER

With an engineering team whose job it is to break down willpower and personal responsibility on the other side of every screen, it's hard for anyone, let alone a twelve-year-old, to maintain a healthy balance. Children are even more vulnerable to screen and gaming addictions. Their frontal lobes are still not fully formed. They haven't yet acquired the ability to stop, reflect on the situation, and take a different course of action. This means they lack the self-regulation and long-term understanding that prevents many adults from developing addictive habits. And it's another reason I tell parents that tech requires parental guidance.

The adolescent brain presents an even bigger challenge. Teen brains are biochemically driven towards three key dopamine-producing behaviours:

- Taking risks
- Trying new things
- Being admired by friends

The roots of this behaviour go way back in our evolutionary history, to a period when adolescent hominids had to venture out into new territories, to find a mate, and help maintain the survival of our species.

These days the new territories are online, but the environment isn't necessarily less treacherous. I was once asked by a journalist to explain why teens would do something so foolish as the "Tide Pod Challenge," one of 2018's most alarming social media sensations. That year, you'll remember, some teens began recording themselves biting into brightly coloured laundry pods, resulting in a spike in poisonings. I told the reporter that the viral challenge fed all three of the teenage brain's unique drives: it was risky, it was new, and posting it led to likes and retweets.

SHOULD KIDS BE TARGETED THIS WAY?

If your kids are anything like mine, they've been 100 percent seduced by social media or gaming platforms at one point or another in their young lives. The persuasive features of technology work especially well on young, still maturing minds. In 2017 an internal company report revealed that Facebook can identify the exact moment when teens feel "insecure," "worthless," or "need a confidence boost." In the document, which was leaked to *The Australian* newspaper, Facebook was actually *bragging* to advertisers and investors about their ability to exploit teenage vulnerabilities.

The intrusion of technology is unravelling age-old traditions and disrupting ways of living that have kept us healthy, happy, and strong. Consider the following:

- The rate of non-screen playtime among children has plummeted by 25 percent in the last twenty years.
- Younger children now spend five and a half hours each day in front of screens, according to studies by the Kaiser Family Foundation, an American non-profit.
- For teens, the figure is more than seven hours (figures that don't include schoolwork).
- Adolescents are now spending more time using social media and playing video games than they are sleeping.
- The average child spends more time communicating through screens than they do face to face.
- In 2008, one year after the iPhone hit the market, people spent an average of eighteen minutes on their phones every day. By 2019 it was up to a daily three hours and fifteen minutes.

But even in my field, child psychiatry, few of us are asking about the ethics of all this. Psychology and neuroscience—fields we tend to associate with healing and helping, ruled by the primary ethical principle of "do no harm"—are being weaponized to pull kids away from homework, sleep, and the crucial developmental work of learning, problem solving, and mastering real-world skills.

Not many industries are as cutthroat and unregulated as big tech, whose decision making clearly doesn't factor in children's well-being. So, in the absence of governmental oversight, parents need to step in.

Former Tech Execs Speak Out

Nowhere is the growing understanding of the problems associated with smartphones and social media more intense than in the San Francisco foothills where they're being created. In the last few years, former high-ranking employees of all three Silicon Valley behemoths, Google, Apple, and Facebook, have begun blowing the whistle on their products, warning especially of their effects on children.

Now forty, Sean Parker describes himself as "something of a conscientious objector" against social media, which "literally changes your relationship with society, with each other," he says. "God only knows what it's doing to our children's brains."

Chamath Palihapitiya, former vice-president of user growth at Facebook, has similarly come out against social media. As he puts it, the "short-term, dopamine-driven feedback loops we've created are destroying society." He says he feels "tremendous guilt" for the role he played. Of his own children, Palihapitiya added, "They're not allowed to use this shit."

None of the Silicon Valley reformers have been louder than Tristan Harris, a former product manager at Google. Harris has spent the past several years encouraging people to get off the technologies he helped create. His non-profit organization, the Center for Humane Technology, includes a team of former tech insiders and CEOs who "intimately understand the culture, business incentives, design techniques, and organizational structures driving how technology hijacks our minds." The "ultimate freedom" is "a free mind," says Harris. "We need technology that's on our team to help us live, feel, think, and act freely."

Still, the reality remains: tech companies have a deeply unfair advantage over parents, few of whom even realize the seductive power of these devices and how easily they can colonize their kids' lives. Tech evangelists tend to remind us that we've seen this outbreak of parental panic before. Telephones, radios, and even books induced serious concern among parents, teachers, and authorities when they were first introduced. TV was initially derided as a "vast wasteland" that was making kids "aggressive and irritable." But TVs weren't constantly tweaked to make them more and more addictive. As Harris notes, "It's *Homo sapiens* minds up against the most powerful supercomputers and billions of dollars." It's like bringing a knife to a space laser fight, he adds. "We're going to look back and say: 'Why on earth did we do this?'"

Meanwhile, several Asian governments have taken action. Both South Korea and China have introduced so-called "Cinderella" laws that force young gamers to log off. South Korea's "Shutdown Law," enacted in 2011, bars anyone under sixteen from gaming between midnight and six a.m. In 2019 Beijing announced its gaming curfew in the belief that video game addiction was to blame for the rise in nearsightedness and poor academic performance among young people. Chinese gamers under eighteen are now barred from playing online games between ten p.m. and eight a.m. The new rules also limit those under sixteen from spending more than two hundred yuan ($29) per month on add-ons like virtual costumes, pets, and weapons.

IDENTIFYING MEDIA ADDICTIONS

The WHO's 2018 decision to add gaming disorder as a diagnosable disease was not without controversy. The way we initially understood addiction was through substances like alcohol, cocaine, opioids, and other drugs. Whether gambling, a *behaviour*, can be addictive was hotly debated for two decades in the psychiatric profession before behavioural addictions were added to the *DSM-5* in 2013.

The debate over the WHO's classification began when researchers began documenting the same brain changes in gambling addicts as in people who were addicted to drugs: their heart rates spiked and they sweated when they couldn't gamble.

Addiction boils down to compulsively seeking something out despite the negative consequences. Addicts show an inability to cut down their consumption; since they develop a tolerance over time, they need higher and higher levels of stimulation for satisfaction. Additionally, they experience cravings they cannot control.

So when I'm trying to explain tech addiction to parents, the first thing I suggest they do is look for the presence of the following:

- **Craving:** Thoughts, feelings, and bodily sensations or cravings to participate in the behaviour
- **Loss of control:** Lack of control over gaming or internet use
- **Compulsion to use:** Increasing priority given to the gaming or internet use over other activities to the extent that it takes precedence over other interests and daily activities
- **Use despite the consequences:** The continuation or escalation of gaming or internet use despite the occurrence of negative consequences such as failing an exam, neck strain, weight gain, or loss of sleep

For example, if your child is staying up until three in the morning gaming even though it means he won't be able to function at school the next day—and his report card reflects it—it is time to intervene.

Keep in mind that the pattern of behaviour must be so severe that it's harming personal relationships, it's interrupting schooling, sports, and other activities, and it's been evident for at least twelve months. But I wouldn't wait for major negative consequences or a year-long pattern to develop. Watch for signs of addiction in your child no matter their age, and intervene early. As well, consider common risk factors for addiction in general:

- Family history of addiction
- Mental health disorders such as anxiety, depression, ADHD
- Peer pressure to use or to participate in problem behaviour
- Family disconnection
- Early use
- Prior challenges with an addictive drug or behaviour

HELP YOUR YOUNG GAMER FIGURE OUT WHY THEY'RE GAMING

Don't be afraid to ask your child all the reasons they think they're gaming. Help them understand that while sometimes they're doing it to have fun, other times they're doing it to check out from the world, or to escape anxiety or depression. This is the first step towards helping your child. Once you understand *why* they're playing for hours on end, you can suggest new habits and a new routine that might satisfy the underlying motive for it. Even if the solution doesn't come easily, the first step is understanding what the behaviour was rewarding in the first place. Consider the profiles below and how you can help your child depending on which one they may fit.

- **The lonely gamer** who's using gaming to socialize might benefit from cultivating new social ties. You could help him find a club or an activity where he might make new friends.
- **The bullied gamer** who's using gaming to escape from teasing or bullying might benefit from school intervention, assertiveness training, or even a martial arts class that might help her build confidence.
- **The bored gamer** who's using online games for entertainment might benefit from a different type of cognitive stimulation, like reading novels or learning a new sport. Try brainstorming ideas or sitting down with your child to watch documentaries or movies that are interesting, funny, or take you to new worlds together.

WHAT THIS MEANS FOR OUR CHILDREN

When it comes to addiction, anxiety, depression, and other mental health issues, there's always been the chicken and egg debate: Did the depressed person discover that drugs or alcohol helped numb their pain, leading to addiction? Or did the alcoholic become depressed because their drinking problem caused their life to spiral out of control? It's often difficult to separate the two.

The data shows that about 70 percent of youth with an addiction also have a mental health issue, and vice versa. Very few people with a diagnosed addiction don't also have a mental health issue, whether it's anxiety, depression, ADHD, PTSD, an eating disorder, bipolar disorder, or something else. The science supports the "common cause" conception, meaning that the problems start from the same place and run in parallel with one another.

The data also clearly shows that an adolescent with a mental health problem or an addiction vulnerability is at a higher risk of developing an addiction to tech. And in general, we know that the seeds of addiction are sown in childhood and adolescence. With a tech addiction, this occurs through two mechanisms:

1. **Repetitive use.** This primes the brain to repetitively seek dopamine, or a high. In turn this creates the neural pathways that become stronger over time, and soon the habit (dopamine hit) becomes a dominant trail in your child's brain.

2. **Repetitive use of tech as a coping skill.** The young person becomes reliant on short-term pleasure to escape from negative emotions. This prevents the development of neural pathways required for healthy coping with stress, sadness, and other negative emotions.

DOPAMINE FEEDBACK LOOP

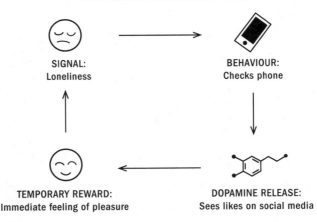

SIGNAL:
Loneliness

BEHAVIOUR:
Checks phone

TEMPORARY REWARD:
Immediate feeling of pleasure

DOPAMINE RELEASE:
Sees likes on social media

Given that addiction is a disease of neural plasticity, the repetition aspect is essential. It occurs when the trail, or neural pathway, forms a strong loop between an external association, like checking social media, and a brief, internal feeling of pleasure or a short escape from anxiety.

Parents may unwittingly allow the addiction to spiral out of control by allowing the anxious child to connect with friends online or to relieve exam pressure through gaming. The problem is, self-medicating with tech is no better than using marijuana or alcohol to cope. The precious young people in our lives need support, guidance, and sometimes treatment to help them deal with the underlying problem. When they do, these behaviours tend to become much more manageable or even disappear.

YES, I'M AFRAID WE DO NEED TO TALK ABOUT PORN

For most parents, internet porn is an uncomfortable topic. Denial, naïveté, stigma, embarrassment, and shame are just some of the reasons keeping them from bringing it up with their kids. Other parents, some dads especially, tend to think their sons' use of porn is a normal part of growing up. They might remember dirty magazines or images getting passed around when they were teenagers. The experience today, however, is completely different from what earlier generations saw. Online porn today is more graphic, more visual, and more disturbing, and is sometimes live.

When he was in grade six, my son was shown scenes from a graphic movie. It deeply upset him, and took him several days to recover from it. I like to remind parents that once your child sees these images they can't un-see them.

My son is hardly alone. In a recent study led by Indiana University's Center for Sexual Health Promotion, 36 percent of teen boys reported seeing videos of men ejaculating on women's faces, one-third of boys and girls had seen BDSM (bondage and discipline; dominance and submission), and 26 percent of males and 20 percent of females had seen double penetration. Another problem with online porn is that some adolescents are using it as a how-to guide. And some teens have trouble distinguishing what's real from what's fake. A 2016 British study showed that 53 percent of boys and 39 percent of girls thought pornography was "realistic."

Online porn is also reaching kids at a younger age than most parents realize—and the impact can be devastating. I've seen many adult men in my practice who say that their use of porn during adolescence has ruined their lives.

Others are encountering it by accident: a young boy might be Googling "anaconda" and end up on a porn site, as my son did. This is similar to how Alexander Rhodes, a Pittsburgh web developer and the founder of an anti-porn website, was himself first introduced to porn. He grew up in a home full of computers; his dad is a software engineer and his mom is a writer. When he was eleven, Rhodes mistakenly clicked on a banner ad and found an image depicting rape. He was intrigued and kept clicking.

That initial curiosity eventually evolved into a daily devotion to hardcore pornography. The compulsion became an addiction, which saw him masturbating to porn as often as fourteen times a day: "I was relying on pornography as some kind of emotional crutch," Rhodes says. "If anything bad would happen, you would go to porn because it would always be there."

Sooner or later, however, those who use escapism to avoid deal-ing with their problems have to return to reality. If kids don't deal with their deeper issues, they don't simply disappear. And the more time they spend in a fantasy, the less energy they have for dealing with their real-world issues. Whatever they're doing to numb their feelings and mask their pain risks becoming addictive.

Porn addiction and porn-induced erectile dysfunction are hot topics among psychologists, psychiatrists, and researchers. These diagnoses haven't yet been recognized by the medical establish-ment, but I believe they soon will be. We're seeing children become desensitized to violent sexual imagery—and we know that there's a connection with difficulties establishing relationships and a heightened tolerance to arousal.

A lot of young men who've gone through puberty using internet porn are reporting a decreased interest in seeking out sexual part-ners, difficulty achieving arousal during sex, and an inability to achieve an orgasm without porn. Rhodes argues that one can see more women in a few minutes online than a primitive man likely saw in a lifetime. The resulting "super-stimulation" has behavioural con-sequences similar to what drugs, alcohol, or gambling can do to the brain's reward centre. Indeed, a 2014 University of Cambridge study using brain imaging showed that the porn-addicted brain reacts to porn cues the same way the drug-addicted brain reacts to drug cues.

By the time Rhodes was in university, he had what he calls "porn-induced erectile dysfunction." He was dating for the first time, and could maintain an erection during sex only by fantasiz-ing about pornography. Nothing quite worked when he focused solely on his girlfriend. That was the turning point. "I was at a low point and seeking answers to why I felt such a slave to this."

In time, he finally quit the porn habit and decided to help others, founding the porn-recovery platform NoFap ("fap" is a slang term for masturbation). The site is aimed at men looking to escape pornography. It offers a counter that tracks exactly how many days a person has abstained, with badges awarded for such milestones as going a week, a month, or a year without masturbating to porn.

I strongly believe that we need to sound the alarm on this topic. We need to educate parents on the serious effects of online porn, and add it to digital safety curriculums in a much bigger way. There needs to be a public discussion about and recognition of porn addiction, with professional treatment similar to what gamblers or internet gaming addicts receive to help return the brain's reward centre to normal. We've already lost too many promising youth, mostly men, to the darkness of internet pornography.

THERE'S HOPE FOR TEENS WITH ADDICTIONS

Kyle, the young man with a full-fledged addiction to gaming, agreed to enter recovery. But for his mom, Michelle, finding the appropriate treatment for him was an exercise in frustration. In Asia—a hub of video game creation, use, and addiction—treatment facilities aimed at helping uncontrollable gaming have existed for years. In North America, however, gaming rehabilitation centres are hard to find, and demand for the existing programs is high.

Michelle initially considered sending Kyle to a residential recovery program near Seattle, but the first seven weeks of care cost $30,000. Its wait list was several months long. Then Michelle found Last Door, a residential treatment centre in New Westminster, B.C., just outside Vancouver, which specialized in media addictions and charged two-thirds less. I've directed many patients to Last Door over the years. For some, it really is their last option.

And for Kyle, as for many of my patients, Last Door turned out to be a godsend. When he arrived he'd been living in his parents' basement, "using every day, suicidal, and totally incapable of living my life." He wasn't using for pleasure. He was gaming so that he wouldn't feel worse, he explains: "It was a survival mechanism." When he walked into his first meeting, the group of six patients, all young men, began chanting *"One of us. One of us. One of us"* and patting him on the back. He felt accepted. During that meeting Kyle began hearing some of the other guys talking about things he'd been feeling for years—and, for the first time, he started to feel hopeful.

He was barred from electronics—he'd be sent home if caught using. Gradually, he was taught how to socialize and exercise. At Last Door, patients help run the household. Kyle took a job in the kitchen, where he learned to cook and to eat more healthfully. And slowly, as he found a new way to live, he felt the desire to use slip away. The depression that had tormented him for years began to lift.

After leaving Last Door, Kyle went back to school and eventually became a high school mathematics teacher. He got a job three hours from where he lived with his parents and has since earned a master's degree that will allow him to become a school principal. He's been clean for five years now.

Often, the best way to overcome an addiction or a bad habit is to initially replace the original behaviour with another habit or even a distraction. When Kyle reflected on his gaming addiction he saw that it was the interaction with other players that helped soothe his loneliness, so he overcame his addiction in the long run by cultivating a vibrant social life and taking a job as a teacher that brought him meaningful extended relationships. He attends three Narcotics Anonymous meetings per week and helps run the local NA chapter. He's had a girlfriend for almost a year, and recently took her home to meet his sister and parents. "I shouldn't be alive today, let alone living this incredible life," he says.

When it comes to potential addiction, early action is always best, but even if your child is further down the path, it's never too late.

REMEMBER . . .

- Dopamine works by filling us with a sense of pleasure and excitement. Anything we do that triggers the release of dopamine is something we'll want to do again and again—to feel that rush of pleasure.
- Dopamine is the key neurochemical of addiction.
- Facebook's Sean Parker has admitted that the platform was designed not to connect us but rather to addict and distract us. Many other tech executives are speaking out.
- Many social media platforms and video games are designed to trigger dopamine release. The most successful techniques hook us by exploiting deep-seated human needs—for social approval, novelty, and social reciprocity, among others.
- When an online service is free, you're not the customer, you're the product.
- In 2018 the WHO added gaming disorder to its International Classification of Diseases (ICD-11).
- Children and teens are especially vulnerable to screen and gaming addictions because they have an immature frontal lobe and have trouble with long-term planning and self-regulating.
- The teenage brain is uniquely driven to take risks, seek novelty, and gain peer admiration.
- Addiction is often a result of repetitive habits or a means to self-medicate and distract from an underlying mental health issue such as anxiety, depression, or ADHD.
- Internet porn is an uncomfortable topic, but it's reaching kids at a younger age and more profoundly than most parents realize.

SOLUTIONS

In this chapter we've been discussing how the pleasure/reward neurochemical dopamine can have negative effects on behaviour when inappropriately released in the brain. We know that dopamine is released when we hunt, gather, and bond to reward activities important for our survival. We've also seen the darker side of how tech companies are designing their products to overload us with dopamine and keep us coming back for more.

In the pages that follow you'll find suggestions for how to introduce and monitor your child's personal device, minimizing the risk of addictive technology and avoiding behaviours that may make your child more susceptible to other kinds of compulsive behaviours later in life. In addition, this section will present some of the signs and symptoms of addiction to watch for and give you strategies for weaning your child off the tech that may be taking over their lives.

KEY STRATEGIES

DON'T

- Assume that no harm will come to your child because "everyone else is doing it"
- Worry or believe your child needs tech at a young age to "keep up"
- Give your child a personal phone or tablet
- Get addicted to tech yourself

DO

- Introduce tech as you would car keys
- Scaffold and support healthy digital habits
- Increase privileges and independence one step at a time
- Watch for tech misuse and addiction
- Intervene early if signs appear

AVOID . . .

Guide your child away from any tech that leads to a dopamine rush or feelings of intense pleasure. This includes online gambling and pornography. Avoid it as much as possible, for as long as possible.

LIMIT AND MONITOR . . .

Avoiding video games and social media entirely is probably not realistic. Unfortunately, almost all have some component of persuasive design. Thus, parents need to oversee their use, especially in the beginning. Discuss, limit, and monitor video games and social media until your child seems to understand the manipulation methods and can regulate their own use.

HOW TO INTRODUCE A PERSONAL DEVICE TO HELP
FOSTER SELF-REGULATION

You'd never just hand the car keys to your child without first having conversations, driving lessons, and practice on local roads before highways. Similarly, we shouldn't be handing over powerful addictive technology to children without first teaching them how to safely use it. As they grow older and demonstrate more understanding, responsibility, and skill, let them progressively access more tech.

So when you introduce a phone or a laptop computer, establish clear parameters with your child. Give them increasing responsibilities as time goes on, following the plan below. Don't forget to continue to monitor and help with their social, emotional, and time management skills every step of the way.

Above all, there's one big suggestion I encourage parents to follow: please, please, *please* don't *give* your child a phone or computer. Don't make it a birthday gift or Christmas present. If you like, you can buy a phone for their personal use. But be clear that it's *your* phone, that they're allowed to borrow it, and that you can take it back if things don't work out. The same logic applies to an Xbox, Nintendo Switch, or whatever else will be the next console or tablet to come down the endless pipeline of expensive technology devices. It's important to establish that you control the supply lines.

Before Handing Over the Device . . .

- Have a conversation with your child in which you're clear about what the device is to be used for.
- Establish house rules, using some or all of the ideas below.

- Carve out screen-free areas of the home (kitchen table, car, bedroom) and maintain daily screen-free times (family meals, homework time, reading, bedtime).
- Notifications and autoplay must be turned off on all devices in the home.
- Choose one day of the week when no one uses devices.
- Shut off Wi-Fi—ideally two hours before bedtime and until your child is off to school the next morning.
- Set up a family charging station in an open area like the kitchen, where everyone plugs in their devices when they're not in use.
- Let your child know that, at first, you'll need all passwords and will be checking their phone regularly. The sooner they illustrate responsible use, the sooner they gain privacy and independence.

In the Early Days of Use . . .

- Devices should be used to communicate with parents, teachers, and friends for practical issues like homework or the carpool. They may text friends to find out about an assignment, but not to socialize. In the beginning, socializing is best conducted in person.
- Don't allow social media, video games, or streaming apps like Netflix. The use of these apps is a privilege that must be earned. Tell them that using those apps is like driving on the highway. First you have to learn to navigate the local roads.
- Keep an eye on your child's time management, emotional regulation, and social skills during this early period to ensure that they have control over their behaviour.

Once They've Shown Competency with the Basics . . .

- Give them a few more privileges—the ability to communicate with friends in a chat group, for example.
- Maintain limits on their usage, and if your child wants more time, ask them how they plan to manage that time and self-regulate their use.
- As their privileges grow, check in with your child, asking them to print out their browser history and discuss what they're seeing, or ask them what media they used and discuss how they felt about it.
- Give your child some responsibility to help guide younger siblings, cousins, friends, or neighbours. Teaching others is a great way to solidify their own knowledge or mastery.
- Expect mistakes! Setbacks are inevitable, and part of the learning process. This is where a break from the phone is a good idea.

WHAT TO DO IF YOUR CHILD SEEMS TO HAVE A TECH ADDICTION

1. Know the Risk Factors

You might have a gut feeling that your child's relationship to the digital media in their life may be harming them. Studies suggest that those prone to addiction may have the following identifiable risk factors. Does your child have any of the qualities that might predispose them to addiction?

- Difficulty creating and maintaining relationships with their peers

- Frequent feelings of social isolation or loneliness
- Mental health issues such as anxiety, depression, ADHD, or psychosis
- Impulse control problems such as anger management or attention deficit
- Addictions, such as alcohol, drugs, shopping, sex, or gambling problems

If you see some of the above risk factors in your child, it doesn't necessarily mean they're struggling with addiction, but it does mean that they could have a higher chance of developing addictive patterns in the future. Use this knowledge to inform the way you monitor their tech use, and pay close attention to their behaviour.

2. Observe for Signs and Symptoms

The next step is to observe for signs and symptoms. With tech addiction, there are many physical and behavioural signs you can keep watch for to determine whether your child's usage might teeter into more problematic territory. In addition to the telltale signs of addiction we discussed earlier in the chapter—craving, loss of control, compulsion to use, and use despite the consequences— check to see whether your child is exhibiting any of the following symptoms of tech addiction:

- Eyes glued to the screen
- No natural movements over a prolonged period of time (neck bent down, stiff posture, no change when nudged)
- Resistance to putting screens away

- Angry or defensive reaction when someone comments on their behaviour
- Delaying the basics of life, such as food, water, movement, exercise, sleep, real-life social connection, and even elimination
- Negligence of personal care (brushing teeth, showering, etc.)
- Family conflict over screens
- Withdrawal from previously enjoyed positive activities
- Social isolation
- Feelings of anxiety or depression when they're away from screens
- Constant thinking about getting back to screens when they're away from them
- Taking steps to hide the extent of internet or gaming use

3. Talk to Your Child in a Calm, Collaborative Way

Talking to your child is a great way to learn more about how they feel about their own technology use. And when you approach them in a calm, collaborative way, with genuine interest, and really listen to their responses, you might be surprised by some of the things they'll tell you. If your child appears to have trouble with self-regulation and you want to learn more, try asking some of the following questions:

- Do you find you're thinking about gaming/social media more than you'd like to?
- Is it hard not to play/use even though you may not want to (for example, you want to do your homework but you're craving to game/check social media)?
- When you can't play or be on social media, do you find yourself in a bad mood, anxious, irritable, or bored?

- When you're in a bad mood, do you turn to the screens to solve your problems?
- Do you stay on screens for longer periods of time than you mean to?
- Do you try to decrease your screen time over and over again, only to fail?
- Do you have any physical symptoms from being online so much (backache, eye strain)?
- Do you have any problems with your school or extracurriculars due to your screen use?
- Do you have any problems with relationships with family or friends due to your screen use?

If you've identified any risk factors, or observed signs or symptoms of addiction, or your child has answered yes to any of the above questions, I strongly suggest further evaluation, ideally with a health care professional. If you feel you're confronting a problem with addiction—or potential addiction—read on to learn more about how to help your child reduce their tech use.

HOW TO HELP YOUR CHILD COME OFF ADDICTIVE TECH

Many parents tell me that the most important step in helping their child was simply making the decision to do something in a firm and compassionate way. They worked hard to balance love with limits and firmness with flexibility, wrapping loving arms around their child while removing devices from the home. We kept our Xbox at my husband's office for many weeks the summer *Fortnite* came out, eliminating the temptation to play—and that one act ended a lot of family conflict, restored balance to our home, and possibly thwarted a future issue with addiction.

As an addiction psychiatrist who's worked closely with children, teens, and young adults for over twenty years, I wholeheartedly believe that addiction can be overcome—especially in young people. It's a highly stigmatized and misunderstood phenomenon, which accounts for some of the barriers to treatment. Yet time and again, I've seen young people persevere as parents step in, families come together, and brains rewire. Early intervention is highly effective, so please don't hesitate to discuss your concerns with a professional, even if you feel they may be overblown.

If you're concerned about overuse of addictive technology, try using my six-week, six-step plan (page 242) to help your child evaluate their tech habits and rebalance their use. In more extreme cases professional help will be required, but whether your child is gradually reducing the use of problematic tech or coming off it cold turkey, they'll need your support. In general, it takes the average person ninety days of consistent change to rewire a habit. Thus, it could take three months of hard work for your child to fully come off an addiction to gaming or screens. After that, things will get easier, but they will still need support to stay in control and resist the triggers of regular life.

Before you get started, remember to do the following.

Ask for help: It's hard to treat a true addiction without professional help or intensive peer support. A counsellor, family doctor, or psychiatrist may be helpful in assessing for any underlying medical or mental health issues, and will be an essential support if you have concerns regarding safety (suicidal thoughts, self-harm), violence, running away, and any mental health issues that may be co-occurring. Be open to such approaches as residential treatment, one-on-one counselling, group therapy, and medication. I often prescribe children and teens a variety of therapies and non-addictive medication for withdrawal, addiction, or mental health treatment, and it can be very helpful.

In particular, online porn or gambling addictions are best managed with the help of specialized treatment professionals (as I mentioned earlier in my discussion of porn). There are a variety of specific interventions for each, and a professional in your area can help you find the best option for you.

Expect withdrawal symptoms: Withdrawal symptoms are the opposite of a high. Explain to your children that if tech is helping them relax, cope with stress, or connect with friends, they may initially feel more anxious, stressed, agitated, and disconnected as they come off that technology.

Find peer support: Peer support was such an essential part of Kyle's and Alexander's recovery because it's highly effective. Finding other people who are experiencing the same issues will help your child deal with feelings of shame, guilt, and anger. They'll hear valuable stories of, and ideas about, what worked for recovery and what led others to relapse. Most importantly, they'll have access to a group of people who understand them and can provide support along the way.

Change the environment: Depending on the severity of their addiction, it may be hard for your child to remain in the same environment owing to the triggers it holds. So it may be helpful to change that environment. You might try changing or reorganizing their bedroom or the basement and removing the problematic technology from the home if you can. You might also consider having them stay temporarily with a relative or close friend. Your child might benefit from weekends at grandparents, and if it's summertime, you might take advantage of a sleep-away camp. Getting involved in a previously loved hobby or sport or finding a new one can also help immensely.

I once had a patient whose triggers included the smell of pizza, his basement, hip hop music, and certain clothing. Any of these would lead to cravings. We had to change his basement bedroom, detox him from all screens for two weeks (other than monitored homework), then slowly, over three months, reintroduce healthy, productive screen time in a new environment.

Reintroduce tech under close monitoring: After the withdrawal period is over, your child will need help creating new habits for all the emotions and situations in which they previously relied on tech. For example, if they used tech to cope with stress, they'll need to learn coping skills (page 118). Your child will also need help staying off their well-worn neural trails (their old habits) that are craving to be used. Again, education, professional help, coping skills, peer support, recreational activities, and time are essential for their staying clean while you reintroduce technology in a slow, closely monitored way.

4

STRESSED: Cortisol and Moving Your Child from Survival Mode to Growth Mode

All that we are is a result of what we have thought.

—LORD BUDDHA

"EVERYONE IS ALWAYS on their phones—on the school bus, during break, even in class," my thirteen-year-old patient Chen recently told me, describing how lonely school had become. "No one talks anymore," she added. "Ever."

At lunch, Chen sits with her best friends. But they rarely speak, she says. Like the other teens and tweens at their middle school, they spend the break glued to their phones, silently swiping left and right, opening and closing TikTok, YouTube, and Snapchat, smiling at the dramas soundlessly playing out on their glowing screens.

Checking social media is the first thing Chen does when she wakes up in the morning, before she even goes to the bathroom. And it's the last thing she does at night as she's scrolling herself to sleep. She spent almost the entire summer before grade eight in her room, curled up in bed with her phone, swiping, liking, posting, commenting. She barely saw any of her old neighbourhood friends.

She didn't have time for them. Her online social life had become all-consuming.

This is middle school in the smartphone era.

IS SOCIAL MEDIA MAKING YOUR TEEN FEEL STRESSED AND LONELY?

Of all the tech trends that have shaped the world in recent years, few have had a larger impact than social media. And perhaps none have had such a dramatic impact on the mental health of adolescents. When it was first emerging, social media seemed to offer a space where everyone could share in one another's experiences. But what began as a dream of a more connected world has, for some young people, led instead to feelings of exclusion, stress, crippling loneliness, anxiety, and depression.

Growing up in the 1980s, my friends and I would occasionally comment on how we wanted a better body after seeing pictures of celebs in bikinis on TV or pop magazines. Some Mondays, I wished I'd been invited to that fun party over the weekend that everyone seemed to be talking about. But there was a limit to how much I could see and hear about what the cool kids were up to. I still had my small group of friends, and we'd all walk to the local 7-Eleven during lunch, laughing and bugging each other. With social media, though, today's teens can endlessly obsess over their classmates' adventurous vacations, their fit, beautiful bodies, the latest fashions. They often can't help it, especially when their Instagram feed is filled with fake and filtered photos and their friends and classmates spend lunch and breaks staring into their phones.

I've already mentioned the acronym that captures this very phenomenon: FOMO, or fear of missing out—a kind of silent suffering that comes from witnessing the great times your friends and peers are having without you. The ready access to our friends' filtered lives leads us to compare our drab existence to the false glamour of everyone else's life. Social media helps exacerbate painful feelings of exclusion, loneliness, insecurity, scarcity, and even shame to levels that most adults have never experienced. Yet few teenagers have developed the emotional resources needed to cope with the onslaught of FOMO and the insecurity that often comes with scrolling through their social media feeds.

On social media, spaces where people are forever comparing themselves to others, the messages young teens are too often internalizing are distressingly familiar:

- Everyone is smarter than I am.
- Everyone is prettier than I am.
- Everyone is more popular than I am.
- Everyone is richer than I am.
- Everyone is happier than I am.
- The list goes on . . .

This type of thinking will often leave young people feeling bad about themselves, anxious about their imperfect clothes, parents, friends, social lives. They worry that their night out or vacation pics won't measure up. The space also enables a sense of false intimacy and a worrying lack of accountability. You can delete someone. You can disappear. The community feels real until suddenly it's not. It can leave you feeling empty and alone.

Chen, my patient in middle school, tells me she no longer feels like a kid anymore. In grade six, when all her friends had phones with Snapchat and Instagram—even though none of them were above the thirteen-year-old age limit the sites require of users—she stopped doing everything she used to love: skipping rope at recess, building forts, playing with slime, doing cartwheels on her lawn. When she started seeing me later that year, she was dealing with some very adult problems, including FOMO, anxiety, depression, and suicidal thoughts.

Fifteen years ago it was still rare for me to see patients as young as Chen exhibiting suicidal behaviour. But these days, she's no longer an anomaly. I have a half-dozen patients her age, some even younger.

The data supports what I'm seeing in my practice in Vancouver. In the last decade, rates of depression, anxiety, body image issues, suicidal behaviour, and self-inflicted injuries like cutting have rocketed upwards, especially for girls aged ten to fourteen. This mirrors a worrying uptick in these behaviours for older girls. The effects of social media aren't limited to girls, of course, but since they tend to be the primary users of social media, its consequences are more pronounced among them. And as the typical age when kids get their first phones has fallen to ten, we shouldn't be surprised to see children Chen's age, members of what's known as Generation Z, beginning to exhibit psychiatric problems. In the sections ahead, I'll explain why.

WHAT IS HAPPENING TO GEN Z?

Jean Twenge, a professor of social psychology at San Diego State University and a leading expert on generational differences, began noticing abrupt shifts in the behaviours and emotional states of adolescent girls. At first, she and other researchers thought these were blips. But the trends persisted across several years. And, as she writes in her book *iGen*, in all her analyses of generational data—some reaching back to the 1930s—she'd never seen anything like it.

Twenge was initially skeptical of those blaming internet use for all that ailed Generation Z: it seemed "too easy an explanation for negative mental-health outcomes in teens, and there wasn't much evidence for it," she writes. But the more she looked for explanations, the more she kept returning to two distinct, apparently unconnected trend lines: the rise in adolescent mental health problems and smartphone adoption.

The sudden spike in rates of loneliness, depression, and suicidal behaviour in girls began in 2012. This happened to coincide with the moment smartphones reached market saturation, with more than 50 percent of Americans reporting owning one. The U.S. data also showed steep declines in the number of hours teens were spending with friends and romantic partners:

- Roughly 85 percent of both boomers and Gen Xers went on dates when they were in grade twelve. By 2015, just 56 percent did.
- In the late 1970s, 52 percent of twelfth graders got together with their friends almost every day. By 2017, just 28 percent did. The drop was especially pronounced after 2010.
- Among twelfth graders, 39 percent said they often felt lonely in 2017, up from 26 percent in 2012.
- And 38 percent said they often felt left out in 2017, up from 30 percent in 2012.

Just when teens began spending more time on their phones and on social media and less time with their pals IRL, alarming trends in adolescent mental health were being noted not just by researchers but by psychiatrists like me. This change was far more pronounced in girls than in boys:

- Depression in teen girls increased by 50 percent between 2012 and 2015. In boys, the jump was 21 percent.
- Suicidal behaviours in girls have increased by 70 percent since 2010. For boys, the increase has been 25 percent.
- Over the last ten years, 62 percent more girls aged fifteen to nineteen were admitted to hospital for self-harm.
- For girls in the ten-to-fourteen age group, hospital admissions spiked by 189 percent.

These trends aren't limited to teens. University-aged young adults have also been impacted:

- The proportion of incoming first-year students who reported feeling "overwhelmed" rose to 41 percent in 2017, up from 29 percent in 2010.

Depression and suicide clearly have many causes, and so understanding why adolescents are suddenly battling disturbingly high rates of loneliness, anxiety, suicide, and depression presents a challenge to researchers. They can point to correlations, but not to causes. Still, the fact that these were massive jumps that occurred over a relatively short time frame helps narrow the potential causes.

Anxiety and depression existed long before Instagram. But the round-the-clock responding to Snaps, posting to social media, and obsessively following the beautiful, filtered exploits of their peers isn't something Gen Xers had to cope with. Even millennials didn't have to learn how to deal with this new reality until they were young adults.

I've started treating very young female patients with body image disorders, anorexia, and bulimia. And I believe selfie culture is a big part of the reason for this. It brings more exposure and more scrutiny to girls at increasingly young ages. By the time they're ten, children are starting to congregate on social media. And unless you've got rock-solid self-esteem, are impervious to jealousy, and have an extraordinarily rational capacity to remind yourself exactly what everyone is doing when they post their glories on social media, it's difficult not to care. In her book *The Happiness Effect: How Social Media Is Driving a Generation to Appear Perfect at Any Cost*, Donna Freitas calls Facebook the "CNN of envy," a kind of "24/7 news cycle of who's cool, who's not, who's up and who's down." Social media may be just one factor, but it's clearly playing a role in declining adolescent mental health.

GIRLS ARE FROM INSTAGRAM, BOYS ARE FROM XBOX

Most kids growing up today are attached to their screens. But as some of the stats I cited above suggest, when it comes to problem tech use, there's a clear gender divide. And while social media is having an outsized impact on girls' body image and rates of depression and anxiety, boys are far more likely to develop media addictions, especially to video games.

As we saw in the preceding chapter, developers know that teenagers have a developmentally skewed drive to gain admiration from peers through abilities and accomplishments, which is why they build rewards into games, like coins, cash boxes, and levelling up—carefully curated hits of dopamine that keep boys playing games for hours on end. And as these games are becoming more advanced, more immersive, more social, and more mobile, rates of gaming addiction among boys are soaring.

Gender isn't binary, of course, and girls, too, are at risk of developing gaming addictions, just as social media can make boys more susceptible to depression and other problems. But these research findings help us understand the risk factors for depression, self-harm, suicidal thinking, general misery, and loss of potential.

THE STRESS RESPONSE

The first thing to understand is that stress is an excellent thing when our life is threatened—and toxic when it's not. Adolescence is already a period of potential intense stress. The way teenagers respond to toxic tech is adding even more to the already hefty stress load they're coping with. The other thing to know is that adversity is a natural part of their lives. New experiences, transitions, deadlines, and pressure can all evoke feelings of uncertainty, anxiety, overwhelm, and dread. Learning to cope with this and with life's ups and downs is an essential part of growing up. Suffering, however, is not.

Have you ever wondered what's going on inside your child's mind as they scroll through social media or go down the rabbit hole of a first-person shooter game, all the while growing more remote, irritable, and stressed out? Your child's brain is constantly scanning the environment for threats and communicating with other systems of their body and mind to determine how to handle them. When your child's brain perceives a threat, it sends an alarm signal to the two walnut-sized adrenal glands sitting above the kidneys. Akin to suddenly flooring the gas pedal, this signal induces a surge of adrenalin and cortisol—the body's natural emergency sirens—that allow the body to spring into action with a burst of energy. These two hormones activate the fear centre to try to protect us from danger.

Adrenalin works in the short term, while cortisol's effects are longer lasting. Adrenalin causes our children's hearts to beat faster and divert blood in preparation for the "freeze, fight, or flight" response I talked about earlier. This is the body's protective response to stress, and it's designed to help your child respond to imminent danger. Their breathing will quicken and become shallow and their blood sugar levels will rise as they prepare to deal with a threat. The short-term release of adrenalin is actually good for your children—when, and only when, they're facing danger. It increases their vigilance and energy levels, improves their memory, and redirects blood flow to fuel their muscles, heart, and brain. Every human body on the planet reacts similarly when they sense a threat.

STRESS IN RESPONSE TO A LIFE-THREATENING SITUATION = A HEALTHY RESPONSE

- **Freeze:** Your body is telling you to stop, hide, and listen for a bear in the bushes.
- **Fight:** Your body is telling you to fight off an angry dog that's biting you.
- **Flight:** Your body is telling you to run fast to escape the tiger chasing you.

Although the occasional release of adrenalin and cortisol to avoid danger is key to your child's survival, a sustained release of the hormones associated with the stress response can have serious consequences on their physical and mental health. Over time, excessive cortisol release can lead to poor sleep, anxiety, and depression. It can also lead to a suppressed immune system, intestinal problems, muscle wasting, reduced bone formation and stunted growth, and disruption of the brain's developing architecture.

Humans, unique among the species, have evolved a "thinking brain"—which is why we're the only species that can trigger the stress response through our thoughts alone. I like to compare the way the brain works to a computer operating system. In a stressful situation, when your brain is suddenly flooded with cortisol, it seizes up the way a computer sometimes does when you have too many windows and programs open. Then comes the annoying blue spinning ball (freeze). That causes you to get angry (fight). Or, you turn it off and walk away (flight). In short, we don't need an actual life-threatening situation to send us into survival mode. We can think ourselves into releasing adrenalin and cortisol by scrolling through Instagram, by playing a video game, or just by being distracted all the time. And in the context of our day-to-day lives, this is an unhealthy stress response.

STRESS FROM THOUGHTS ALONE = AN UNHEALTHY RESPONSE

- **Freeze:** Your mind reacts to stress with anxiety, procrastination, avoidance, and indecision.
- **Fight:** Your mind responds to stress with irritability, anger, rage, or passive-aggressive resistance, including oppositional behaviour or stubbornness.

> • **Flight:** Your mind reacts to stress by mentally escaping, either through distractions—repetitively checking social media, playing a video game, shopping online—or using a substance.

Although today we've experienced far fewer famines and wars than in centuries past, a shift in societal values and unhealthy lifestyles has increased stress levels. And in the long term, stress can kill us by activating diseases like mental illness, heart disease, and cancer. This is why the WHO has declared stress the number one health epidemic of the twenty-first century.

SURVIVAL MODE VERSUS GROWTH MODE

The human body comes equipped with a complex web of nerves known as the *autonomic nervous system*. It regulates our heart rate, breathing, blood pressure, and more. This system has two components.

The *sympathetic nervous system* prepares the body for an intense physical reaction to respond to a threat. We're said to be in "survival mode" when this system is activated. All the body's energy is diverted to help us freeze, fight, or flee in order to survive. When we're in this state, it's not possible for us to grow, learn, recover, adapt, or innovate.

These activities can occur only when we're in "growth mode," when the *parasympathetic nervous system* is activated. This system can function only when we're not stressed. It works best when we're feeling relaxed and calm.

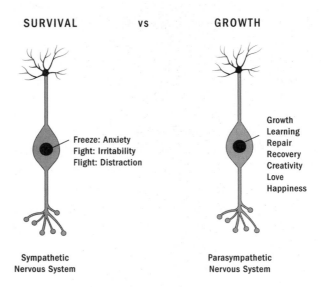

SURVIVAL   vs   GROWTH

Freeze: Anxiety
Fight: Irritability
Flight: Distraction

Growth
Learning
Repair
Recovery
Creativity
Love
Happiness

Sympathetic
Nervous System

Parasympathetic
Nervous System

Young people start running into serious problems when they repeatedly trigger their sympathetic nervous system (and go into survival mode) for reasons that aren't life threatening. That is, when they experience chronic, daily stress.

Certain apps, games, and websites are constantly triggering anxiety and fear in your children—that they aren't cool enough, pretty enough, skinny enough, witty enough. That they're missing out on a hangout or were deliberately not invited. These constant spurts of the stress response are flooding developing brains with toxic levels of cortisol.

This repeated triggering is also building stress as a habit by strengthening its associated neural trails. As we've learned, the more neural trails are developed, the more easily triggered they can be. Remember, the pathways your children walk on create the lives they lead.

On top of that, "hyperarousal," an abnormally heightened state of anxiety, suppresses the brain's frontal lobe, the area where mood regulation takes place. This state of heightened arousal makes it hard for young people to control their feelings. They might become anxious and indecisive (freeze). Or they might lash out at Mom when she tries to limit their screen time (fight). Or they might turn to obsessive gaming, or social media use, or substance use (flight). These are all reactions to stress. They're signs of a brain under too much strain, and they need to be addressed.

Even though checking out and distraction have practically become the norm, these aren't healthy responses in daily life. When your child is checking out, they're not actually processing their thoughts and emotions; they're repressing or avoiding them. They're in flight mode. They miss out on the chance to identify, understand, manage, and communicate how they feel. This is known as "emotional regulation," and it's an essential life skill that's linked to health, happiness, and success.

Repressed emotions can lead to more stress and more distraction. Eventually, the child who uses tech to cope with life stress can become overwhelmed with anxiety, anger, and distraction, and will have trouble coping with real life. Their grades may drop; they may lose interest in sports. Their relationships can suffer.

TECH AND HIDDEN STRESS

In addition to FOMO, social comparisons, poor time management, loneliness, distraction, and body image disturbances, there are many common behaviours associated with tech that we may not associate with stress.

But the behaviours listed below can indeed trigger the stress response in your child, especially when they engage in more than one simultaneously, which is often the case when kids are using technology. These behaviours can trick your child's brain into *thinking* they're responding to a threat, thereby tripping the sympathetic nervous system. Some of them—being sedentary, say, or not making eye contact—may not seem obviously stressful. However, you have to remember that your child's paleolithic brain doesn't know the difference between sitting for prolonged periods of time in a cave or sitting for prolonged periods of time playing a video game. Their neurons just know that they're not moving and wonder why. Is there a predator nearby? A hurricane coming? This sends a loud signal to their system: *Danger!* The brain mistakenly believes it must be under threat and initiates the stress response.

LITTLE-KNOWN STRESS TRIGGERS

- **Sleep deprivation:** Our neurons don't realize that we're staying up all night because we're on the internet. They think there's too much danger around to sleep.
- **Sedentary behaviour:** A twelve-year study of more than twelve thousand people recently found that those who spend most of their time sitting are 50 percent more likely to die earlier than those who sit the least, even after controlling for age, smoking, and physical activity levels.
- **Sitting crouched or hunched over a laptop:** Our rounded shoulders and flexed neck signal to our neurons that we're hiding from danger in a cave.
- **A lack of eye contact:** Our neurons don't know why we're isolated and not seeing any other people. We must be in danger!

WE HAVE TO DEAL WITH NEGATIVITY BIAS, TOO?

As if all this weren't enough, teens also have to deal with the built-in human negativity bias: the tendency to focus more on the negatives than the positives. If you've ever found yourself dwelling on an insult someone levelled at you, a mistake you made at the office, a fast-approaching deadline, or a tough conversation you need to have, you've experienced the phenomenon. Simply put, negative events have a much larger impact on our minds than do positive ones. It's why social scientists have found that it takes five compliments to make up for one criticism. And this negativity bias has a powerful effect on behaviour and decision making.

It makes evolutionary sense to focus on the potential for problems, especially when there are sabre-toothed tigers wandering around the veld. It's what wired our brains this way. The problem is, the more we walk on these "negativity trails," the greater our risk of developing negative thinking habits, also known as "thinking traps." I've listed some of the more common ones below. If you have a teenager, you might want to review them together. I'll bet you recognize each other in them!

Mental filter: You filter out the positive and focus only on the negative. For example: You post a new photo to Instagram and receive ten compliments. The one snarky remark is the one you focus on.

Jumping to conclusions: You interpret things negatively when there are no facts to support your conclusion. For example: You assume your friends are angry with you because no one has texted you recently.

Black and white thinking: You see things as all or nothing—there's no in between. For example: If you don't get enough likes on your new Facebook profile pic, you conclude that the photo must be ugly. You don't consider that it's a Sunday afternoon, that your friends might be out enjoying the sun, and that many have deleted Facebook.

Overgeneralization: You see a single negative event, such as not being invited to a chat group, as a never-ending pattern of defeat. You use words like "I *never* get invited" or "I'm *always* left out."

Mind reading: You tell yourself that someone is thinking negatively of you or reacting negatively to you. For example: You interpret a one-word text as an insult.

Personalization and blame: You hold yourself responsible for something you can't control. For example: You blame yourself when your best friend isn't invited to another friend's chat group.

We all know from experience that although negative emotions like fear and anger can well up in seconds, they tend to dwell within us far longer than positive ones. Now think about your experiences online, where outrage and extreme content often tends to dominate—where discussions often veer into emotionally charged territory and where social media feeds leave us feeling left out and anxious. Positive stories aren't the ones getting eyeballs. As computer scientist Cal Newport writes in *Digital Minimalism: Choosing a Focused Life in a Noisy World*, "For heavy internet users, repeated interactions with this darkness can become a source of draining negativity—a steep price that many don't even realize they're paying to support their compulsive connectivity."

STRESS VERSUS CHALLENGE

Don't get me wrong. I don't expect your children to grow into adults without seeing any negative content or experiencing adversity. And some of that adversity will serve a purpose in their lives. For while chronic stress, originating from the lower brain region, is bad for young, developing brains, challenges are not. They push children to think, strategize, and experiment in new ways. And it's through this type of thinking, activated by the higher cortical regions, that they learn to problem solve their way through obstacles. This is why repetitive challenges are good for kids.

STRESS VS CHALLENGE BRAIN ACTIVATION

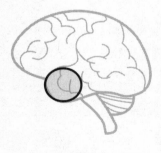 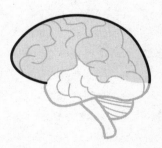

STRESS   VS   CHALLENGE

The best way to challenge a child is to guide them to pursue activities within their "challenge zone," the sweet spot nestled between what's too easy for them and what's too hard. Such activities engage their prefrontal cortex, the brain's most evolved brain region; it's known as the "thinking centre." Easy tasks don't engage your child's thinking centre very much. Tasks that are too hard, meanwhile, can trip the brain's limbic system, or "feeling centre," triggering the stress reaction. The challenge zone is where learning and neuroplasticity occur. This is where children cut new neural trails in their brains. This is where the magic happens.

WHY ARE CHALLENGES GOOD FOR KIDS?

- They release dopamine, rewarding your child with a burst of pleasure.
- They release serotonin, flooding them with feelings of confidence and happiness.
- They activate and work out their brains' frontal lobe—the thinking centre, the area involved in important cognitive skills like judgment, memory, language, emotional expression, planning, goal setting, and problem solving.
- They strengthen the brain in the same way that running or cycling strengthens their leg muscles.
- They train kids to learn to pivot, adapt, and rebound from failure.

THE LAST THING TEEN BRAINS NEED IS MORE STRESS!

As you may have observed in your own teenager, it doesn't take much time scrolling through social media to throw a sensitive, still developing mind off track. It's important to remember that adolescence also happens to be a developmental moment of peak stress. The brain is sorting out a number of things, among them identity, relationships, and sexuality. So with already so many changes in the average teen's life, engaging with certain tech heightens this period of peak stress to an unprecedented degree.

New research has found that adult and teen brains process information differently. We adults tend to think with our fully developed prefrontal cortex, the rational, thinking part of the brain. (Which doesn't mean we always do, of course.) The prefrontal cortex isn't fully developed in teens, however, which forces them to rely on the emotional, reactive part of the brain. That's why they need practice and help learning to self-regulate (calm themselves down). They need your help to learn and use coping skills, consider alternative actions, and adapt to new and sometimes overwhelming situations.

In teenagers, the connections between the emotional or feeling part of the brain (the limbic system) and its decision-making or thinking centre (the prefrontal cortex) are still under construction. The neural bridge between them hasn't been fully connected. And the limbic system is still dominant. Has your teenager ever had an explosive reaction to something only to later have trouble explaining what exactly they were thinking? There's a neurological explanation for this. The dominant part of their brain took over. They weren't thinking so much as they were feeling and reacting. This is also what makes adolescent brains so much more sensitive to tech use than most of us parents realize.

No matter how well your teen can play soccer or how high they scored in AP Physics, good judgment just isn't something their brains can excel at. Not yet. The cognitive-control networks in their prefrontal cortex are undergoing rapid maturation. Full maturation won't occur until they're twenty-four or twenty-five.

To make things worse, adolescence is a moment of heightened self-consciousness. This is why your teen might seem so easily embarrassed. An adolescent's inner critic is constantly on high alert: *Am I dressed funny? Did I just say something stupid? How can I not know that? Why haven't I done that yet?*

As we discussed in Chapter 3, the teenage brain is biochemically driven by dopamine, the neurochemical of reward, to take risks, seek novelty, and gain admiration from their peers. As kids enter their teens they're looking to strengthen and extend their networks of friends. Once upon a time, primates had to venture outside their tribes in adolescence to find mates, and in crossing the savannah they'd have to fend off any wild beasts they met along the way. The reward for taking chances in such dangerous terrain was novelty, new relationships, sex, and reproduction. Teenage brains are still wired the same way. They still yearn to connect with others in order to gain security, support, comfort.

Often, adolescents do this by taking unbelievably stupid risks to impress their friends or potential mates, or for no obvious reason at all. Whether it's texting while driving, drug use, binge drinking, or unprotected sex, teens take more risks than any other age group.

This is why it's so important to teach kids from an early age about emotional literacy and the ways social media is interfering with their moods and behaviours. Engaging in status competitions is nothing new, and it's especially common when we're young. We compare our looks, our hairstyles, our opportunities, our friends, our successes and failures. We seek approval and affirmation all the time. But young people today are buckling under the pressure to project a false self on social media—happy, perfect, popular, skinny. Because of its outsized impact on their mental health, we need to help adolescents understand how social media is influencing their sense of self and their real-life relationships.

The capacity to think critically and philosophically about the role and influence of technology in their lives will empower young people to make better decisions about how they use it, when they use it, and when to log off.

"I didn't realize how much social media was affecting me," Chen once told me. "I can't imagine living without it. But I also know it's making me crazy."

IS IT TIME TO CTRL-ALT-DELETE?

When parents tell me their kids truly can't log off, whether the problem is video gaming or social media, I suspect that their child's screen use has replaced their ability to cope—and I make it clear that the parents need to intervene. This means removing the screens kids use for coping and developing real coping skills. Sometimes it also means seeking professional help.

I have a fifteen-year-old patient named Brittney with 990 Instagram followers. Like 75 percent of teens, Brittney is also on Snapchat. Since having a low Snapchat score is stressful and embarrassing, she relentlessly Snaps friends, earning points to boost her score. When she first started seeing me, Brittney said she felt obligated to like and comment on all her friends' posts, which took her hours every night.

To Brittney, social media can sometimes feel like a part-time job. It's a gig she aged into by virtue of being a teen in the smartphone era. The brand she's managing is her own. She carefully curates it with funny updates, videos it took her hours to perfect, and Photoshopped pictures of her dog, her bedroom, her new bathing suit, her new haircut, her new girlfriend. This is constantly pulling her away from her homework, conversations with her family, even sleep. The angst that can ensue when she posts something with a mortifying lack of likes can turn Brittney inside out, filling her with anxiety and self-hatred—"Instashame," she calls it.

When Brittney's parents first came to me, they told me they couldn't pry their daughter off the phone. They tried grounding her, taking away her allowance. Nothing worked. When they tried shutting off the Wi-Fi, Brittney ran away from home.

I made it clear that they needed to approach Brittney's phone use as they would an addiction. To recover faster, she'd have to detox from Instagram, Snapchat, and all other social media for three months, both inside and outside the home environment. After that, she'd need to either learn to have a healthy relationship with it or avoid it altogether. That's how she would fire and wire new healthy tech trails and cover up the old ones that were causing her harm.

Don't forget: your kids are looking to you to set boundaries. Parental limits help children understand that they're being cared for and that they can't always get their way. They teach them that they can learn things through time, patience, and maturity that they might otherwise not realize they could. No matter how often children act as if they want to be in control, having too much power can be dangerous and even frightening for them. They intuitively know that they need an adult to be in charge, and they count on their parents to guide their behaviour.

So when you do step in and set firm boundaries around your child's tech use, you may be surprised by the results. I once had a patient named Raj who used video gaming to manage his life's stressors. This slowly turned him into a problem gamer. His parents repeatedly set limits to his gaming that Raj, who was fifteen, constantly broke. He was in real trouble: he was barely sleeping and failing most of his grade ten classes. His social interactions were mostly online, and whenever the family dragged him to a restaurant for a meal he'd complain loudly and misbehave until everyone got angry and upset and they returned home. By that time Raj was spending almost all his time alone in his basement bedroom.

He and his parents were at war. At one point, after an especially bad report card, his mom and dad banned him from his Xbox for two weeks. Late one night, Raj snuck into his parents' room and found the hidden console. When his dad realized he was secretly gaming that night, he went downstairs, pulled the Xbox from the wall, opened the back door, and smashed it against their backyard fence. His mom was terrified: she was sure Raj would freak out, destroy the house in a rage, or run away. She thought they might have to call the police to intervene.

But instead of that anticipated all-out battle, nothing happened. Raj stayed in his room. At first he was steaming mad, but after a couple of hours he said his mind started to clear. He was bored—his parents had long since confiscated his phone—so he started to poke around his bedroom. He picked up a novel, *The Outsiders*, that he needed to read for English class. He read the first few chapters without any urge to play Xbox. He knew he couldn't. It was in a million pieces in the backyard. He was so transfixed by the story that he read until he fell asleep.

The following morning, Raj's parents were braced for battle. However, when he came upstairs for breakfast, the first thing Raj did was thank his dad. "I actually slept," he said. "I feel better knowing I can't play it. I actually wish you'd done that a year and a half ago."

Six months later, Raj's mom told me they'd enjoyed some of the best months they'd had as a family in years.

This family's story isn't unique. In extreme cases like Raj's, the use of strong parental authority (although it could have been demonstrated in a gentler way!) is, in the end, often well received by the child. Most striking in Raj's story are the clear difference between adult and teenage brains and the value of limits and boundaries. Raj had a hard time thinking past the moment; he was using tech to manage his anxiety and irritability and to distract himself from being in survival mode. His father, however, understood the long-term consequences. And by removing the mechanism that drove the vicious stress-response loop, he allowed Raj to find his way back to growth mode.

REMEMBER . . .

- Of all the tech trends that have shaped the world in recent years, few have had a larger impact than social media. And perhaps none have had such a dramatic impact on the mental health of adolescents.
- The sudden spike in rates of anxiety, loneliness, depression, and suicidal behaviour began in 2012, coinciding with the moment smartphones reached market saturation.
- The data has also shown steep declines in the number of hours teens spend with friends and romantic partners.
- Because of tech's outsized impact on their mental health, we need to help children understand how it's influencing their sense of self, their coping skills, and their real-life relationships.
- When it comes to problem tech use, there is a clear gender divide: girls are from Instagram, boys are from Xbox.
- The rational, long-term strategic part of a teen's brain isn't fully developed until they're about twenty-five.
- Stress is needed only to help cope with life-threatening situations.
- Stress leads to the freeze (anxiety), fight (irritability), and flight (distraction) response.
- Your child's body is designed to absorb stress only in small doses and in short bursts.
- You want to help move your children from survival mode to growth mode.
- Teach kids to avoid stress and embrace challenge. These have opposite effects, with challenge improving their health, happiness, and success.
- Challenge is an essential part of a child's life. Stress and suffering, however, are not.

SOLUTIONS

In this chapter we've discussed how your children's bodies are designed to absorb stress in only small doses and short bursts. Technology use, however, can trigger constant stress—whether through sleep deprivation, posture issues, time mismanagement, distraction, FOMO, or the internalizing of harmful messages that they aren't cool enough, pretty enough, skinny enough, witty enough. Such constant stress floods their developing minds with toxic levels of adrenalin and cortisol and builds damaging neural trails that can more easily trigger stress in them as they get older.

In the pages that follow you'll find suggestions for tech literacy that will reduce the stress of technology. In addition, this section will give you strategies to teach and model healthy coping skills.

KEY STRATEGIES

DON'T

- Ignore signs of the stress response, including anxiety, irritability, and distraction
- Let your child use tech to cope with life
- Confuse stress with challenge
- Give in to your own negativity bias and thinking traps
- Model being constantly stressed as a normal part of life

DO

- Discuss the difference between being in a state of survival and one of growth
- Encourage healthy challenges
- Teach your child coping skills
- Fight the negativity bias
- Challenge thinking traps
- Pay attention to hidden stress triggers

AVOID . . .

Guide your child away from any tech that triggers the stress response, whether it's social media comparisons, FOMO, sleep deprivation, or prolonged, hunched-over posture.

LIMIT AND MONITOR . . .

Avoiding social media and technology altogether is probably unrealistic. Discuss, limit, and monitor social media until your child seems able to regulate their use of it without the above issues.

TEACH YOUR CHILD COPING SKILLS

Coping skills are clear, practical tools our kids can use when they're feeling overwhelmed, stressed, anxious, or down. All children need to learn and master coping skills they can employ in any situation to manage and reduce the cortisol-induced stress response.

Here I'll outline the three general categories of healthy coping skills—**downtime**, **others**, and **play**—and explain how to establish their positive behaviour patterns.

1. Downtime

Downtime allows us to settle and feel safe. Simply unplugging, taking a break from life, and breathing can be a very effective coping skill. Teach your child to practise downtime, or "quiet time," by closing their eyes, resting, and letting their mind drift, even for a few minutes, at their desk, say, or in the car.

Deep Breathing

I believe that the single most effective way to reduce stress and move children away from survival mode into growth mode is through slow, deep breathing. We often get into the habit of shallow breathing, the type that reaches only to our middle lungs. Poor posture, restrictive clothing, and stress can all contribute to shallow chest breathing. But when we breathe slowly and deeply, the receptors in our lungs and diaphragm expand from the pressure of the air. This expansion signals to our nervous system that we're okay, which shuts down the stress response and moves us into growth and recovery mode.

Once your child gets the hang of deep breathing, they can do it anywhere and on their own: shortly after waking up, before bed, on their way back from school, or just when they need a moment of peace.

In our family we all practise deep, controlled breathing. You can try the following exercise with your child before encouraging them to do it on their own. When we breathe *with* our children, our bodies get the added benefit of syncing with theirs in a wonderful shared rhythm. If you're doing your belly breathing while sitting up, look into your child's eyes. Smile back at them. Deepen the bond between you by being present.

DEEP BREATHING EXERCISE

This breathing exercise will help anyone of any age to relax. Young children love belly breathing, especially when you place a stuffed animal on their belly and take it for a ride!

- Find a quiet, comfortable place for your child to sit or lie down.
- Teach them to breathe in slowly through their nose and breathe out slowly through an open mouth. Whereas a clenched jaw signals stress to our brain, a relaxed, open jaw (as in a yawn) signals safety.
- When they get the hang of it, invite them to bring the breath slowly into their belly and to feel the belly expand. Then, as they exhale, encourage them to do it slowly and to pay attention to how their belly contracts.
- Start with three breaths and work up to more until your child is fully relaxed.

2. Others

Whether it's a family member, a friend, or even a pet, social bonding helps us feel safe and settled. Spending time with others is a powerful coping skill.

Guide your child to practise meaningful social connection, even if for just a few minutes, by cuddling a pet, FaceTiming with a grandparent, or giving them a good morning or goodnight hug. Make a habit of encouraging one-to-one bonding time with a sibling, a cousin, or a friend. Every one of them will benefit from it!

And try to find an undistracted few minutes alone with your child every day. Trust me, I know this is harder than it sounds! But when we give children our full attention, they can feel how dearly we hold them in our hearts, strengthening our bond with them.

3. Play

When your kids try new things, or spend time on their passions, hobbies, and interests, they activate the prefrontal cortex—thereby moving from survival mode to growth mode. And since play ignites curiosity, exploration, and fun, it inhibits the release of cortisol. After all, the body can't be playing and stressed at the same time. This makes play a great coping skill.

Guide your child to give themselves a daily dose of play, even if it's just for a few minutes. In our family, the trampoline acts as a stress reliever. It's impossible to be stressed—and hard not to smile or laugh—while bouncing away on it. We also love to have dance parties in the kitchen. And we prank one another every chance we get.

TEACH YOUR CHILD TO FIGHT THE NEGATIVITY BIAS

Your child's brain is built to be more sensitive to bad news than good news. But if you can help them learn to see the good things in life at a young age, they'll find it easier to do the same when they're older.

The ability to discern the good alongside the bad is a skill that takes time and practice. Use some of the following strategies to help your child see a situation from all angles.

- Discuss the pros and cons of everyday situations so that they can see both sides.
- Tell them stories of how bad events led to positive outcomes in your life. For example, you may have been passed over for a job or not chosen for a team, but that led to your finding a better job or team.
- When things go wrong, ask your child, "What's the silver lining in this situation?" If they can't yet see it or feel it, ask them to try to imagine what it could be.
- Life's challenges and disappointments most often build resilience, so explain this process when your child is facing a tough time. Tell them that the challenges and obstacles they face are helping to train them in being strong and better able to bounce back.

Challenge Thinking Traps

To help your child deal with negative thoughts, encourage them to face these thoughts directly instead of ignoring or pushing them away. Here are some questions that can help you challenge unhelpful thoughts your child may be having. Ask them as an ally who's standing with them shoulder to shoulder. You can also have fun with the questions and make your child laugh—it's a good way to change their mood.

- What's the worst that could happen?
- If it did happen, what could you do to cope with it?
- Are you falling into a thinking trap?
- What's the evidence that this thought is true?
- What's the evidence that it *isn't* true?
- Have you confused a thought with a fact?
- What would you tell a friend if they had the same thought?
- On a scale of one to ten, how big of a life problem is this?

Teach Your Child to Pay Attention to the Basics

I've talked about the little-known stress triggers that can send our children into a negative state when they're immersed in their screens. Some of these are inevitable, which is why it's important to balance an online life with real-world interactions. Consider the following strategies to help your child combat these insidious stressors.

- **Sleep deprivation:** Remember the sleep guidelines from Chapter 2 (page 43)? Please do try to stick with them. The biggest way to avoid sleep deprivation is to value sleep! It's how our brains rejuvenate, recover, and rewire. Now, I know that what with homework, exams, sports events, and trips away, it isn't realistic for kids to get the required sleep every night, but try to catch them up whenever possible. Parents can guide kids to take naps, sleep in on weekends, and rest more during holidays (I encourage my kids to do all three, and sometimes I even reward extra sleep!). When your kids reach their teens, they can often experience a circadian rhythm shift and have a hard time sleeping at night. To help them, try scheduling in a morning spare.

- **Sedentary behaviour:** Guide your child to get up every half hour and stretch their body. Consider downloading one of the many apps that send a notification when it's time to move.
- **Sitting crouched or hunched over a laptop:** I've put up a poster on our fridge demonstrating good sitting and standing posture. I've also placed Post-it notes, bolsters, and pillows all over the house to encourage good posture instead of the all too familiar text neck, hunched shoulders, and chair body.
- **Lack of eye contact:** Teach your kids to make a practice of looking at people's faces and eyes whenever they speak. When my kids are going through shy phases, I tell them to look at the person's nose.

5

WIRED FOR HEALTH: Endorphins and Finding Balance in an Unbalanced World

There is nothing outside of yourself that can enable you to get better, stronger, richer, quicker, or smarter. Everything is within. Everything exists. Seek nothing outside yourself.

—MIYAMOTO MUSASHI

A few months ago I started seeing a fifteen-year-old patient who'd begun cutting herself with an X-Acto knife pulled from her art supplies. Zara isn't depressed. She doesn't have any addiction issues. She was cutting because she was severely burned out.

Zara is a star soccer player at the club level. Her dream is to play at a U.S. Division I college on a scholarship. (She worships Megan Rapinoe.) Zara is also an excellent public speaker and debate champion. She's a straight-A student, and was named head girl at her school in September. Her parents push her hard. Zara pushes herself even harder.

She's a great kid with some pretty good life skills, but tech has complicated her life and contributed to an overwhelming sense of exhaustion that's making her feel as though she can't keep up.

Zara, like so many other teens, finds herself constantly comparing herself to others, especially online. She may feel great about her soccer skills, but then she'll see on social media that a former teammate is playing a level up. She may be proud of her debate performance, but then she watches YouTube videos from the international debate competition and feels like an amateur.

Zara also wants to be a perfect pal. She feels obligated to like and comment on all her friends' social media feeds. When she receives a notification that a DM or an email has come in she feels compelled to reply, even when she's in the middle of doing homework, watching a TV show, reading a book, or sleeping.

Because of Zara's leadership role at school, her classmates are constantly emailing or texting to ask for help with homework or debate prep or even just for general information. She's also frequently invited to parties, soccer tournaments, and conferences. The other day, as she sat down to do her homework, an invite to attend a We Day youth event came in at the same time as a message from a grade nine girl who was having trouble with her peers. Meanwhile Zara's best friend, who was raised in a conservative family, was coming out as bisexual on Instagram, and Zara felt she needed to show her support and keep an eye on her feed in case her friend received any negative comments. She had a soccer practice that night and a physics exam the following day.

Zara can be cranky and short with her parents. She's been having trouble studying and has been coming up with excuses to skip soccer practice and even some games, something she's never done before. She's never self-harmed before, either. Zara can't seem to explain why she's cutting. All she could tell me was that she wanted to "feel something."

ENDORPHINS

That something was endorphins. I explained to Zara that they're our body's natural painkillers, released when we're hurt or injured. So when Zara cut herself, it was the endorphins released in her brain that supplied the "relief" she was looking for.

We all produce endorphins naturally. They make us feel good after we work out, hug a friend, or take a long, deep breath. They act in the brain's opioid receptors, lessening pain. It's right there in the name: "endorphin" derives from "endogenous morphine," meaning "internally produced morphine." These wonder neurochemicals also lead to increased creativity and mental clarity.

In this chapter we'll explore the power of endorphins and the importance of self-care. When we take care of ourselves we feel energized, exuberant, alive. It really is that simple—so we'll consider the many ways to help children naturally increase their endorphin production. But first I want to turn to the problem plaguing Zara and many others, both young and old.

BURNOUT

In the last five years I've started treating more young people like Zara: overscheduled high achievers who exhibit signs of physical and mental exhaustion: in short, burnout. And if that burnout is left unchecked, Zara, who's also a perfectionist, risks a downward spiral that can include anxiety, depression, and the use of substances like drugs and alcohol to cope.

Not long ago, burnout tended to be limited to frontline professionals like nurses, police officers, paramedics, military personnel, and social workers: people who face unrelenting mental stress and trauma while at work. But burnout—defined by the presence of emotional exhaustion—is increasingly being seen as a serious, widespread health concern. In 2019 the WHO upgraded burnout to a "syndrome" in its International Disease Classification, characterizing it as a state of "vital exhaustion" that includes excessive fatigue accompanied by feeling demoralized and irritable.

As a psychiatrist, I've seen the devastating impact it can have on a person's mental health, their family life, their studies, and their careers. I can only hope that the WHO's recognition will increase awareness of the problem, prompt people to take better care of themselves, and reduce some of the stigma that is deterring some from seeking help.

A lot of young people tell me that the idea of self-care makes them fear their peers will see them as "weak," not "gritty," unable to keep up. But as I tell my patients, pushing through pain and burying discomfort can set you up for a lifetime of misery. Learning how to say no, how to rest, and how to take care of yourself is a sign of maturity and resilience. Reaching out and asking for help are signs of bravery.

TREATING BURNOUT IN YOUNG PEOPLE

I recognized almost all the signs of burnout in Zara. Her technology use certainly contributed to her condition, so I gave her some practical advice that you might want to consider for your own kids as well.

- First, I had Zara turn off all her phone's notifications, including the ringer, email, and alerts for incoming text messages. I had her get rid of the news alerts she was receiving from *BuzzFeed*, plus all the alerts from Instagram and Twitter. She needed to stop her phone and laptop from constantly pinging, distracting, and stressing her out.

- I explained how important sleep is for regulating her mood, clearing waste from her brain, and re-energizing her cells. I encouraged her to try to get nine hours of sleep every night, even when she had a speech to prepare or an exam the following day. Freeing up time from technology helped with that.

- I helped Zara understand that she needs to unplug and make time for solitude every day as a way to recharge—whether she's journaling, taking a walk, having a hot bath, or meditating. Yes, teenagers can meditate! I encouraged her to start and end every day with deep breathing exercises.

- I told Zara to cut herself off social media completely until she's able to use it without comparing herself to others. Remember: online comparisons are toxic. They make young people feel that they're not good enough, flooding their bodies with cortisol.

- We also had to start discussing multitasking and perfectionism— how those behaviours had become well-worn trails in Zara's brain, and how she could step off from them.

MULTITASKING IS A MYTH

Zara's story of burnout highlights two corollary issues young people are facing today, both made worse by the omnipresence of technology: multitasking and perfectionism.

In the digital era we've come to believe that we can complete several tasks at the same time—that this makes us more efficient and counters boredom to boot. But multitasking is a myth. As numerous studies have confirmed, the human mind can't focus on more than one thing at a time. What it can do is rapidly switch focus from one thing to the next. I think of it whenever I hear my husband's "email voice," the semiconscious monotone he takes on during a call when an email has popped up and he's clearly reading it while continuing to talk. My husband might think he's simultaneously performing two tasks, but the reality is that he's simultaneously doing two things badly.

Those who multitask initiate parts of the brain that are irrelevant for the task at hand. They're chronically distracted. Their memory suffers. And although people think that when it comes time to buckle down they can turn everything off and become laser-focused, the reality is that they've developed habits that make that impossible. They've lost the ability to focus on one thing at a time. And as we learned in Chapter 2, when we behave in certain ways over and over again, these behaviours develop into habits that we carry out without thinking.

Like Zara, a whopping 72 percent of teenagers—and 48 percent of adults—feel the need to immediately reply to texts, social networking messages, and other notifications, according to a recent study by Common Sense Media. Another recent study showed that the mere presence of a smartphone, even when it's off, can reduce cognitive capacity in young people, causing what researchers termed "smartphone-induced brain drain." And some 90 percent of undergraduates report feeling "phantom vibrations" from their phones on a biweekly basis.

Although multitasking may give the illusion of saving time, neuroscientists have found that not only does it make us less efficient, but it can also cause us significant stress. Back in our hunter-gatherer days predators were all around us, meaning that the slightest distraction could lead to our death. So when we're distracted—flipping among multiple websites, say, or trying to finish a report with the

TV on—neurons signal to our brain that we're unsafe. This can trigger the fight-or-flight stress response we discussed in Chapter 4. In the short term it makes us anxious, irritable, and more distracted. In the long term it causes mental fog, scrambled thinking, and health issues, and can lead to burnout.

Attention is the foundation for all our cognitive capacities, whether it's the ability to remember, to solve problems, or to simply be present with our children. But tech's constant interruptions and targeted distractions are taking a massive toll on these critical brain functions. In 2015 Microsoft published a study showing that, from 2000 to 2013, the average human attention span shrank from twelve to eight seconds. "Everyone is distracted—all the time," says Justin Rosenstein, a former Facebook programmer. And it's stressing us out—all the time.

A NOTE ON PARENTAL MULTITASKING

I'll admit it: after another hour spent waiting around at yet another drawn-out track and field meet with my son, my phone's siren call can start to seem especially alluring. The truth, as every parent knows, is that there are parts of parenting that can be tedious work. But when we check out by reading the latest mind-boggling news story or catching up on email when we're with our kids, we can start to suffer from what the American Academy of Pediatrics calls "distracted parenting."

The most startling documentation of this modern phenomenon came from the U.S. Centers for Disease Control, which found that, after a long period of decline in childhood injuries, hospitals had reported a 12 percent uptick over a three-year period following the 2007 introduction of the iPhone. More specifically, these hospitals had recorded a spike in kids getting burned, getting concussed, and breaking bones because their parents were distracted by their phones.

But there are less obvious problems linked with parental distraction. I was meeting a friend for coffee recently when I noticed a toddler desperately trying to get her mother's attention—waving her hands between Mom and her iPhone, pulling at it, putting her face in front of it. The scene stuck with me, because what I was observing was an interruption in the crucial conversational duet that occurs between parent and child in the early years of the child's life. That duet is key to speech and cognitive development, and it creates an enduring sense of connectedness between parent and child. The scene also made me think of a 2015 study conducted by the University of Michigan's medical school. When researchers observed 225 mother-and-child pairs eating dinner together, they noted that those mothers who used their devices during the meal weren't nearly as attentive to their kids. They missed emotional cues. And their children, who were less likely to be prompted, ate less healthfully.

The good news is that children are prewired to get what they need from their parents, as I discovered when I tried to work while caring for my daughter, Gia, when she was still a toddler. Any time I'd turn to my phone or laptop I'd be jerked back by her pudgy, reproaching hands. To get my attention, she knew to grab my head and pull it close so that I'd be looking her in the eyes. Evidently the little girl in the coffee shop had learned to do the same thing.

THE PROBLEM WITH PERFECTIONISM

Another problem facing Zara is her perfectionism. She's not alone. A recent study showed that, since 1989, perfectionism among American, British, and Canadian university students has jumped by 33 percent. I wasn't surprised. The study, published in the *Psychological Bulletin*, reflects a topic that often comes up among my colleagues at the medical school where I teach.

In our performance-based culture, we tend to consider people "successful" based on who they are on the outside (a straight-A student, athlete, expensive car) rather than who they are on the inside (generous, loyal, kind). The sheer absurdity of the university admissions process already contributes to unhealthy levels of perfectionism among youth. But more and more I find that my students— who grew up with social media, cultivating curated versions of their lives and achievements—are hitting whole new levels.

It's beneficial, of course, to set goals and high standards for your kids, but there's a difference between healthy striving and perfectionism. Perfectionism arises from such negative emotions as stress, concerns about criticism and judgment, low self-worth, and even self-hatred. It's driven by fear and a sense of scarcity. My perfectionist patients always seem to be searching for something in order to feel complete, to fill a void they feel is inside them. Healthy striving, on the other hand, is based on positive emotions: passion for a task, the love of a challenge, the sense that you're contributing to the world. So while one young person might be driven to become a great hockey player, say, because they worry they'll be judged and criticized if they don't perform in the top ranks, another's drive might arise from a love of the game, the thrill that comes with a win, the sense of connection that teams create, the gruelling, collective challenge of winning a championship.

There are two types of perfectionists. Both are linked to low self-esteem, anxiety, depression, frustration, and conflict.

Internal perfectionists:

- Are self-critical
- Are often motivated and feel pressure to be perfect
- Procrastinate. Obsess over details. Have difficulty completing projects. Because they can never achieve their ideal—perfection—they get stuck in mistakes and develop poor time management skills.

All of this makes it hard to meet their own high expectations. Then they internalize their low self-worth and can become anxious and depressed.

External perfectionists:

- Set unreasonable standards for others
- Judge others
- Criticize others.

All of this tends to lead to conflict.

Perfectionism—along with its corollary, overvaluing the way we're seen and perceived—compromises how we feel about ourselves and the people around us. It can also create paralysis. Since young people's lives are playing out online, in public, more than ever before, children and teens are constantly aware of what their peers are doing and how they measure up.

HAPPINESS CAN COME ONLY FROM WITHIN

For decades now, rising rates of burnout, multitasking, and perfectionism, along with distraction, consumerism, and materialism, have correlated with a rise in mental health problems among young people. Today's university students, for example, score significantly higher on the clinical scales for anxiety, depression, paranoia, and psychopathic deviation. And they value money and status more than ever before. It's not hard to understand how kids who've been fed a steady diet of reality TV, celebrity culture, and social media can develop superficial, skewed views of the world.

My experience with teenage patients has led me to believe that many of today's youth are focusing on who they are on the outside at the expense of who they are on the inside. The emptier we feel inside, the more we tend to focus on the person we project to the outside world. The less internal identity we have, the more we rely on such external attributes as our clothes, trophies, or Instagram followers to feel secure and happy.

In psychology, "locus of control" is the degree to which people feel in control of their lives. An external locus of control means you feel that external circumstances, such as your social media popularity and material possessions, control your life and happiness. These things are unpredictable and often in flux, so people with an external locus of control often feel as though they have little control over their lives. Having an internal locus of control, by contrast, means you believe that your internal state—your own efforts and abilities, or your own sense of peace and gratitude—controls your life and happiness.

So I often ask my young patients: Where do you feel the control centre of your life is—the person you are on the inside or the person you are on the outside?

When a young person needs money and status—things like Nike runners or the latest phone—to feel happy and in control, it suggests that their control centre lies on the outside. The problem is that whatever they have will never be enough. Someone else will always have more. There will always be a void they seek to fill. In other words, they're in survival mode. It can be hard for a child like this to feel good about themselves. They're in a constant state of stress (freeze, fight, or flight). Their ingrown negativity biases are easily tripped. An undercurrent of anxiety, irritability, and distraction gets in the way of their feeling happy. Rather than celebrate being made assistant captain of the hockey team, for example, their minds might fixate on who was named captain.

But when a young person is instead guided by their values and identity, they tend to be less reactive and anxious and less likely to become depressed. They're in the growth mode. If your child's locus of control is on the inside they'll tend to have a stronger sense of self. They'll tend to be happier because they're happy with who they are. And this internal sense of self-love keeps them in growth mode, opening up higher cognitive processes and brain power. Instead of wasting energy on their superficial identity, they focus on such intrinsic goals as health or living a meaningful life. And pursuing these sorts of things releases the endorphins that power our passions, motivation, and creativity.

There's a lot of truth in the old adage *Happiness comes from within*. Money, social status, admission to Oxford—none of it will lead to lasting happiness. True, enduring happiness can come only from inside us, with the help of neurochemicals like endorphins.

TEACH YOUR KIDS THE WARNING SIGNS

The trick is getting kids to pay attention to what's happening inside of them. Easier said than done, I know. Still, try explaining to your children that they were born with a nearly foolproof system that kicks into gear when they're doing something that could cause them harm.

When they feel hunger pangs, their brain is saying *Eat!*

When they feel thirsty, dry-mouthed, and a bit headachy, their brain is saying *Drink!*

When they feel fatigue and their eyes start to close, it's their brain saying *Sleep!*

If their neck and shoulders are hurting from too much video gaming, the message is *Move! Stretch!*

Loneliness is part of that same early warning system. It's telling them *Stop being alone! Rejoin the tribe!*

When your kids forget or dismiss the signals reminding them to do the things they need to do for their well-being, they'll get those flashing lights—insomnia, agitation, irritability, fatigue. And if they continue to ignore those signals, their stressed bodies will release more cortisol and eventually become dysregulated. That's when they can get hit with anxiety, burnout, depression, chronic body pain, diabetes, and addiction.

So it's vital that we teach our kids to pay attention to their internal signals and care for themselves. This is called self-care. Without it, they can get sick. Trust me, I know. I've been there.

WHAT HAPPENS WHEN YOU DON'T
TAKE CARE OF YOURSELF

I was born with a genetic disorder, called Ehlers-Danlos syndrome (EDS), that affects collagen production. I didn't even know I had it until my forties, when I was hit with severe chronic pain. Because my joints are hypermobile and I have poor balance, I've suffered many serious injuries in my life—injuries I never took proper care of. For example, when I was thirty I fell off my bike, shattering my left elbow, shoulder, and parts of my ribcage. After two surgeries and minimal attention to all my injuries, I essentially forgot about the accident for the next decade. Those years were a blur, both professionally and personally—with three pregnancies, moving homes, scientific research, speaking and writing, and building a clinical practice in psychiatry.

A few years after my bike accident we had our first son, Joesh. I was thirty-four at the time and founding director of British Columbia's Youth Mental Health and Addictions program. I'd taken just four months of maternity leave before email, Skype, and an external locus of control lured me back to work when I should have been resting. My career had become too big a part of my identity, and I needed it to feel good about myself. Then, shortly after Joesh turned one, I got pregnant again, this time with Jaever, our second son. During both pregnancies I kept the same frenetic pace—and started having worse back, knee, and general body pain. Doctors started to investigate whether I had lupus, rheumatoid arthritis, and other conditions.

Shortly after the birth of our daughter, Gia, in 2010, I began researching and writing my first book, *The Dolphin Parent*. It sounds crazy, and it was: I was still working as a medical director with administrative, research, teaching, and patient care responsibilities, in addition to having three young children, aging parents, and a deteriorating body.

I was multitasking my health away. I'm still not sure if it was true passion or perfectionism that drove me to work so hard; likely it was a combination of the two. On the one hand, in my practice I felt a deep pull towards trying to counterbalance the dangerous parenting trends—overscheduling, overdirecting, and overcompeting—I was seeing all around me (and that I even found myself participating in). On the other hand, it was not at all a great time to take on such a massive project. However, I just wasn't conditioned to listen to my body or take care of myself. I didn't know how to slow down or even rest.

My body and mind couldn't keep up that pace for long. I knew I needed regular sleep, exercise, and social connections. These are all simple things, but I was having trouble fitting them in. I learned the hard way that knowing isn't doing, and simple isn't easy. In order to juggle a full-time career with my family responsibilities, community service, and friends, I was skimping on all the essentials for a life of health and happiness. As I counselled my patients and audiences to rest, pause, spend time in nature, and laugh, I neglected doing these things myself. I'd forgotten the very basics of life: conscious breathing, enjoying the moment, caring for your body, connecting with yourself and others every day. I didn't recognize it then, but the load was too heavy for me to handle. And it wasn't long before my body let me know.

By my fortieth birthday I was completely flattened by deep, aching, chronic pain. There were many days when the prospect of getting out of bed felt terrifying. I had no idea what was happening—no diagnosis and no medical plan. In my lowest moments, I couldn't see a way out.

Looking back, I believe technology was a factor in making me so sick, but it was also a factor in getting me better. I joined online chronic pain groups and saw patterns in other people's stories that were similar to mine. After five years of searching, I found and ordered my own genetic test online. I spit in a cup, sent it in—and then received the EDS diagnosis.

Finally, I was able to grab the reins again. My first order of business was changing my mindset from hating my body to loving it back to health. I had to stop fighting it in survival mode and start nurturing it in growth mode, and that meant finding balance.

I realized that, to get better, I had to change my body's internal chemistry: I needed to slow the production of stress-related neurochemicals like adrenalin and cortisol and increase the powerful healing of endorphins and others.

I learned to listen to my intuition, the signals I was receiving from the core of my being. In doing so I changed my internal environment from survival to growth, where all healing and recovery occurs. And technology certainly helped me do it.

THE IMPORTANCE OF SELF-CARE

A lot of the messaging our kids are getting from parents, schools, and coaches is about getting a perfect report card, scoring goals, and winning competitions. What they're not being taught, however, is how to take care of themselves. It's critically important to understand that your child isn't here to make you feel proud. She's not here to fix your emotional needs or to replay your childhood. In fact, she's not here for you at all. She's her own person. And so we have to show her how to treat herself with compassion and self-care. She needs to learn to release her own endorphins, not look for dopamine on her phone or be driven by fear and cortisol.

By "self-care" I mean anything your kids do to take care of their mental, emotional, and physical health. This can be as simple as taking a hot bath or going for a walk. It could mean taking time to work on an art project or going to a movie alone. For some, it could mean going snowboarding. For others, it means learning to say no.

Self-care is intensely personal and wildly variable. It's whatever your child does to help them repair, recover, and face the next morning. It always involves tuning in to their own thoughts, feelings, and biology—their intuition. It's about getting out of survival mode and living in growth mode.

Practising self-care hasn't always been easy for me, and it might not be easy for your child, either. I started small, by taking the time to finally get orthotics in all my shoes and going for the occasional therapeutic massage. Later, it meant being honest with myself, my family, and my colleagues about how much time off I needed and actually allowing myself to take that time. Physically, I can no longer put in a forty-hour work week. I have to rest in the middle of the day. I take a heating pad to my office and restaurants. I say no to social events. Now, this was hard for me to accept. After all, self-care isn't something our current society always values, meaning that it's often not easy to carve out the time to look after yourself. So I've had to work on not feeling as if I need to apologize or make excuses for taking time to myself.

Rather than risk letting our children experience burnout, serious illness, or waste away years being exhausted, perfectionistic, and unfulfilled, let's teach them self-love. They need to know that their most important job is to take care of themselves. And guess what? Technology can be extremely helpful in doing this.

In the paragraphs that follow I outline some of the essential behaviours for releasing endorphins and how technology can help foster them. I draw on my own experience, explaining how I learned to increase my body's endorphin production and became a happier, more confident, and more positive person.

Downtime

In Chapter 4 I talked about downtime as an effective coping skill for stress, but it's also an essential part of human life, one that we're losing to busyness and technology.

When I was sick I recognized that if I were ever going to get myself out of the stress-response system I'd need to slow down and get some downtime. But after running on adrenalin through five years of pain—on top of an ADD brain—I found the prospect challenging. So I turned to my phone to help me. I used apps like Calm, which provides the scenes and sounds of nature, among them waves, birds, and falling rain. Humans are "biophilic," meaning we're meant to live in nature. So Calm helped me at the beginning of my journey towards deeper inner work by simply helping me . . . well, calm down.

We need to help our kids understand that their brains need breaks—a bit of space and quiet. It doesn't need to be a long time; five to ten minutes is plenty. But even brief breaks allow their minds to process and make sense of the new information they're taking in every day. And when we don't take the time to do this, it's harder for us to retain that knowledge. Studies of rats, for example, have demonstrated that when they were given time to rest after trying to find their way through a maze, they were far better at remembering its layout than when they didn't rest.

When kids rest, their brains are anything but idle or unproductive. Quieting the mind allows them to affirm their identities and make sense of themselves and their interactions. They might, for example, think back to how they might have better handled a conflict or a tough conversation, preparing them for the next time they face something similar.

And when we look inward our morality emerges. It's when I'm stuck at a train crossing or waiting for the kids to come out from soccer practice that, all of a sudden, I think: *I should call my aunt, she's really sick,* or *I was too harsh in that meeting with my colleague last week. I should check in on him,* or *It's been six months since I last connected with my good friend.* When you're too busy, you're too busy to be kind.

All ancient traditions have valued time for contemplation and reflection, observing such rituals as bathing in hot springs, sitting still with incense burning, and meditation. The Christian grace that's said before eating a meal allows a person time to reflect on the divine. *Know thyself* was inscribed on the Temple of Apollo when it was built in ancient Greece more than three thousand years ago.

Today, though, many people are addicted to being busy—something I know intimately because it once included me. Our society tends to stigmatize those who rest as being lazy. Being busy has become a symbol of importance.

In my work with young people I prescribe them antidepressants to help relieve symptoms of depression and anxiety. I also prescribe them a daily dose of downtime. It's essential for helping them rebuild their mental health. I often encourage my own kids to take a break from whatever task is on their to-do list—to shut down their devices, close their eyes, and let their minds wander.

WHY DO KIDS NEED DOWNTIME?

- To process all the information, knowledge, and skills that young brains are receiving day in, day out. This requires relaxed, unchallenged time.
- To fully synthesize new information and life experiences
- To consolidate memories from the day, revive their focus and attention, and renew their drive to learn
- To give them time and space to learn to manage their feelings
- To learn to cope with boredom

Mindfulness

When I explain mindfulness to my patients, I tell them it just means being actively present in the moment. It means being keenly aware of yourself and your surroundings. It means connecting with your physical senses—seeing, hearing, tasting, smelling, and touching—as well as your internal senses of feeling and thinking. Over time, I tell them, it will help reprogram their minds to think in healthier ways.

When your kids practise mindfulness, they're redirecting neural activity from the reactionary part of their brains (the survival system) to the feeling and rational part (the limbic system and the prefrontal cortex). In doing so, they're training themselves to react less to impulses, to slow down, to think and feel before they act.

The opposite of mindfulness is multitasking, the scattering of our attention that leads to stress. When we're focused our brain gets the signal that we're safe, which helps keep us calm and centred. But when we're distracted, constantly shifting our focus, our brain believes we're in trouble and will launch the freeze-fight-or-flight response.

The research shows that mindfulness not only enhances emotional regulation, helping kids feel more present, calm, and engaged, but that it also improves cognitive performance—including when the stakes are high. As well, mindfulness has been shown to help improve attention and behaviour problems and to reduce anxiety in kids. In a 2013 study, an eight-week training in mindfulness improved concentration and significantly reduced hyperactive behaviours in boys with attention deficit hyperactivity disorder (ADHD).

The power of mindfulness is finally being understood in our mainstream culture, too. Schools across the world are teaching it. In Vancouver and India, my Dolphin Kids programs teach children as young as three years old mindfulness, breathing, meditation, and social skills. And once they get the hang of these practices, I can tell you that children of all ages love it.

Meditation

Okay, I know there are still some meditation skeptics out there. The research, though, is overwhelmingly clear. I can cite the science until the moon comes out, but by now you've probably already heard the long list of meditation's benefits: it's been shown to lessen stress, depression, anxiety, pain, and insomnia. What you might *not* have heard is how it may affect children. Here are just a few examples specific to kids.

- Meditation improved the behaviour and self-esteem of children with ADHD, according to a 2004 study.

- Eighty-three percent of kids from low-income families reported feeling happier, more relaxed, and stronger with a meditation practice, according to a 2015 study.
- University students who briefly meditated scored higher on attention tests after just five days, according to a 2007 study.

People say that meditation is the most difficult thing they've ever tried. Sadly, I have to agree. Learning to resist distraction is the hardest habit I've ever changed, and a daily meditation practice was by far the hardest habit I've ever developed. But nothing has served my well-being more.

I remember meditating alone in our basement one dark winter morning when I suddenly realized that, for the first time in six years, I didn't feel any pain. I'd completely forgotten what that was like. It was life changing: after months of a daily practice I'd changed the neural trails I'd been running on. In other words, I'd finally been able to shut down survival mode and move to growth mode. I was actually producing endorphins on my own.

Not long after that, I decided to stop taking opioids to help with my pain. I even shot a video to mark the moment when I emptied my final bottle into the toilet. I spent the next seven days in withdrawal: I was nauseated; my head pounded; I sweated through the night. But I got through it.

By that point I'd spent years trying to get pain-free from the outside. The experience profoundly changed me, both as a physician and a person. Before all this I'd been a traditional, Western-trained doctor who separated body and mind. These days I'm much more holistic—and passionate about helping my patients understand the connection between their bodies and minds.

Laughter

A good laugh, I've learned, is a great start to the day. Our kids have made crowding into our bed, sometimes with an iPad, a fun part of relaxed weekend mornings. We queue up videos of Stephen Colbert and Lilly Singh. Seeing Joesh, Jaever, and Gia rolling around in the covers in a fit of giggles over the latest hilarious meme gets me laughing right along with them. Indeed, research has shown that we're thirty times more likely to laugh in the presence of others than alone. It's like a yawn, triggering the feel-good receptors in the brains of people around us. I like to think of it as a game of endorphin dominoes, spreading happiness.

DILLON'S STORY

Dillon Hill knows all about the healing powers of laughter and bonding. When he was in grade five in California, his best friend and classmate, Chris Betancourt, was diagnosed with Stage 4 chronic myeloid leukemia. Dillon's hospital visits with his friend felt pretty awkward; they were only ten, after all. They didn't have the emotional maturity to process what was happening. All that changed when Chris's dad brought in his son's PlayStation 2. Soon it was like old times again. The pair were laughing and joking and having a blast together. Playing video games brought some normalcy to a profoundly abnormal situation; it helped Chris forget about the frightening reality of his hospital room. The experience bonded them for life. "Cancer is life-changing for fifth-graders," Chris told *USA Today*. "It made us more than classmates."

Years later, when they were in high school, it also inspired them to form a non-profit charity called Gamer's Gift. The pair raised money to bring video games and virtual reality devices to hospitals and assisted living facilities to help alleviate some of the stress and loneliness patients may be feeling.

Music

The human brain evolved through music and dance. All cultures share a love for both; they light up our brain and body with stress-relieving, healing, joyful neurochemicals. And both have been among the few constants in my life. As a teen I started using music to help me focus, and I'd dance to ease my stress and have some fun. I listened to music as I studied for finals, for the Medical College Admission Test (MCAT), and for every other exam I've ever written. When I entered medical school at nineteen my ADD and stress was at its worst, meaning my headphones were always blaring—Nat King Cole, Aretha Franklin, nostalgic Bollywood songs, Boyz II Men, George Michael, Whitney Houston, Prince. I don't think I could have become a doctor without music.

When my illness hit me six years ago, I knew I needed to get my mind and body out of sick mode. Remembering the power of music, I turned to it. You and your children can use music to bring stress relief, bonding, and joy to your lives, too. Some of the most joyful moments of my life have been dancing in the kitchen with my family.

Exercise and Sleep

When your kids exercise or get a good night's sleep, they experience feelings of well-being, contentment, and even joy. When they don't get enough sleep, however, they feel tired and irritable—their little bodies think they're in distress and so release stress hormones that can, as you now know, wreak havoc on their minds and bodies.

Research has repeatedly shown that those who work out, even for as little as ten minutes a day, tend to be more cheerful and upbeat than those who never exercise. And active people have a much lower risk of developing depression and anxiety than those who are sedentary.

Once I understood my prognosis, I made sure to build healthy amounts of sleep and exercise into my daily routine. I started counting my steps with a Fitbit, gradually increasing them, and using my iPhone to help me track my daily activities, mindfulness, and sleep.

Gratitude

I was eleven the first time I remember feeling a wave of gratitude wash over me. I was visiting India for the first time with my mother, who'd taken me to the Golden Temple in Amritsar, a sprawling, hectic city near the Pakistan border. The Golden Temple—the holiest shrine in Sikhism—is an elaborate complex of marble and gold set in the middle of a sacred lake. And like every Sikh temple, it contained a free kitchen, or "langar," that provides handmade meals around the clock to all who enter. This one had been operating for over four hundred years, serving as many as a hundred thousand people every day—all by volunteers! I was helping my mom in the kitchen when I met a group of skinny, rag-clad, barefoot homeless kids who lived on Heritage Street, just behind the temple walls.

I felt a rush of colliding emotions: guilt, fear, and sadness, all at the same time. I also realized how lucky I was to be growing up in Canada, how full and easy my life was by comparison. Which isn't to say it was perfect: my parents were struggling immigrants with not a lot of money and many responsibilities; the stress weighed on both their health and their marriage. But in that moment in Amritsar I felt intensely grateful to them for the herculean sacrifices they were making to provide us with a better future—one that so many can only dream of. I carried that perspective with me back home, and to this day it propels me forward.

There's a lot of research showing that gratitude can positively affect our moods and general well-being, and that grateful people are happier and less stressed overall. Studies have repeatedly shown that simply expressing gratitude—even if you're faking it!—can measurably improve a person's overall happiness and life satisfaction.

Making gratitude a daily practice has been essential to my recovery. A few years ago I started keeping a gratitude journal to help remind myself of all the good in my life—my three amazing (if exhausting) children, my (occasionally) patient husband, my (messy) home. Sometimes, of course, it's hard to be entirely positive when you're feeling upset or just not well. Yet those are the times when you need gratitude the most. On the hard days when I start worrying about my pain, I listen to gratitude affirmations from YouTube before going to bed. It helps ease my feelings of anxiety and sadness relating to my prognosis.

Recently, and for the first time, I delivered a talk to an audience of several thousand people. Before I walked onstage I took a few seconds to myself in the green room to give thanks for what I was about to do. Beneath my dress I was wearing a hip brace, a knee brace, and a thoracic belt. I'd put on a black leather jacket to hide the bulky straps. There was a time when I would have been ashamed of my disability and my limitations. But as I walked onstage that night, I felt grateful, courageous, and alive.

Getting sick helped me realize that I'd forgotten the basics of living a healthy life—practising deep, controlled breathing, turning inward, downtime, mindfulness, laughter, sleep, exercise, and gratitude. And I'm not alone in this. I firmly believe that the frenetic pace of our technologically driven twenty-first-century life is leading to epidemics of stress, burnout, loneliness, and the chronic diseases that plague Western society. I recognized that I'd become so busy multitasking and overachieving that I'd thrown my life—and my kids' lives—off balance. I'd stopped making my own endorphins and was running on cortisol. I was flattened by this reality, suffered for years, and worked hard to build myself back up. It wasn't easy. But once I did I was struck by how kind and generous nature is to us: when we honour our biology, we are rewarded. It's an important lesson to teach our children: when you know yourself and love yourself, you can heal yourself.

REMEMBER . . .

- Endorphins are the body's natural painkiller, stress reliever, and bliss molecule and protect us from burnout, pain, and illness.
- Endorphins act in opioid receptors in the brain to make us feel a rush of well-being when we work out, laugh, or take a long, deep breath.
- Burnout is a state of emotional exhaustion. It comes from depleting our biological systems by running on stress and cortisol for too long.
- Technology has made distraction, multitasking, and perfectionism much worse, contributing to burnout and other physical and mental health issues.
- Locus of control is a psychological concept that identifies where the control centre of your life is. Individuals who depend on external attributes and events to feel good about themselves are prone to unhappiness. Those who believe that who they are on the inside matters most do better in life.
- Our performance-based culture can contribute to children developing an external locus of control, needing more, never feeling good enough.
- When children go inward, listen to their bodies, and practise self-care (such as exercise or getting a good night's sleep), their brain's motivation centres light up from the wave of endorphins.
- When they're distracted, don't listen to their bodies, and lack self-care, they feel tired and irritable.
- Mindfulness, meditation, laughter, music, and gratitude encourage the mind to think in healthier ways, reducing stress, depression, anxiety, pain, and insomnia and improving memory, problem solving, creativity, and overall happiness.

- When kids rest, their brains are anything but idle or unproductive. Quieting their mind allows them to affirm their identities and make sense of themselves and their interactions.

SOLUTIONS

In this chapter we explored the power of endorphins and the importance of self-care. Endorphins, you'll remember, are released when we slow down and take care of ourselves by taking breaks, being mindful, and being grateful, for example. Your children can naturally produce endorphins. The neurotransmitters make them feel good after they run around outside, laugh out loud, or meditate. When your children connect with themselves and practise self-care they feel energized, exuberant, alive.

In the pages ahead I'll outline a series of tactics you can use to guide your kids towards self-care. These practices will help counter the increasing trend of burnout and the twin scourges of perfectionism and multitasking. I'll also encourage the kinds of technology use that foster downtime, self-care, and endorphin release.

KEY STRATEGIES

DON'T

- Overschedule your kids' lives
- Show your kids love only when they perform
- Compare them to others
- Focus on who they are on the outside (awards, grades, athleticism) at the expense of who they are on the inside (kind, honest, creative)
- Forget that they're always watching what we do

DO

- Celebrate efforts over performance
- Focus on progress, not perfection
- Love your kids for who they are
- Help them set realistic goals
- Fight perfectionism by talking about your own failures and what you learned from them
- Guide your child towards practising self-care

AVOID . . .

Multitasking is toxic, so avoid it at all costs! When using tech, it's important to focus on one task at a time. Remember to keep talking to your child about avoiding falling prey to online comparisons and FOMO.

LIMIT AND MONITOR . . .

Any technology used mindlessly, without a clear purpose. With this kind of usage, the flight response of distraction will suck away important time and energy.

HOW TO RECOGNIZE BURNOUT IN YOUR KIDS

For adults, burnout mostly relates to excessive or prolonged stress, whether in the home or at work. In children, though, it occurs when they face ongoing stress or just busyness with little chance to relax and recharge. Here I've listed some signs of burnout to watch for. You'll see that many of these behaviours reflect the stress response: freeze (anxiety), fight (irritability), and flight (avoidance or distraction).

- **Procrastination:** Your child used to race to do his homework after school. Now you have to keep reminding him until he sits down to do it.
- **Avoidance:** He used to love soccer and taekwondo. Now he comes up with all kinds of excuses to avoid going.
- **Being late:** His positive attitude has disappeared. He's often late to school or to practice.
- **Trouble concentrating:** He's constantly distracted and can't sit still for longer than a few minutes at a time.
- **Snappishness or testiness:** These days, everything seems to upset her.
- **Negativity:** He constantly makes negative comments about activities he used to love.

- **Apathy:** She doesn't seem to care about things the way she once did. When you used to ask her about gymnastics class, she'd tell you all about what she learned. Now she just shrugs and says "It was fine."
- **Anxiety and fearfulness:** Preparing for science and math tests was never easy for her, but she's suddenly super anxious about tests, to the point where it's causing her to lose sleep and have nightmares.

SELF-CARE FOR KIDS

The best way to prevent and manage burnout is with self-care. Remember the coping skills we learned in Chapter 4—downtime, others, and play (pages 118–20)? These activities are actually much more than just coping skills. When used every day as a practice, the same activities become tools for self-care, health, vitality, and peak performance. A daily dose from all three categories will keep your child in growth mode, helping them feel motivated, confident, and creative. If possible, help your child create a quiet, personal space where they can go to practise some of these techniques. Often, technology can help! The more they practise, the more skilled they'll become.

Biofeedback

Biofeedback is a powerful technology tool kids can use to get to know themselves, whether it's figuring out how much time they're spending sitting, on their screens, and sleeping or how their heart rate changes when they breathe deeply or play a violent video game.

My kids use Apple's Health app and Fitbits to track steps, heart rate, and sleep quality. The app can also track nutrition, menstrual cycles, and body measurements. There are countless technology devices that can provide valuable biofeedback for things like posture, mindfulness, and meditation.

Breathing Practice

As I mentioned in Chapter 4, deep, controlled breathing is one of the most powerful coping skills your children can acquire. However, if you want them to do more than just cope, guide them to practise breath work daily for peak performance. This stretches the receptors that signal safety and activate the parasympathetic system.

Breath work can also be a wonderful metaphor when encouraging your child to develop a new mindset towards life. Just as it's impossible to avoid or hold on to your breath for more than a few seconds, the same is true for the inevitable changes in life. Eventually you have to let go.

Yes, Kids Can Meditate!

There are many ways to meditate. Some are based on ancient practices, others on modern science. The cool part is that throughout the ages and across the world, the basic technique of meditation has remained the same: Still your mind. Move from thinking about the past or future to being in the present.

There are countless apps that provide some basic theory and offer mindful minutes and guided meditations. These can be a great place to get started. Don't expect your child to fall into a blissful meditative practice right away. The key is to begin—and to try a little bit every day. I suggest first thing in the morning or last thing in the evening, for logistical reasons: it's quiet, and there are fewer interruptions. A comfortable space that's free of distractions, such as a bedroom or office, works best.

Encourage Journaling

Evidence shows that writing down your thoughts and feelings helps to improve your mood and reduce anxiety and stress. Many of the children and teens I work with love to write or draw in a journal or diary. These are deeply personal and private, so consider taking your child to buy one (or help them make one) that appeals to them. Tell them that it's theirs and that you won't read it.

I've shifted my own practice from writing things down to voice dictation straight into the notes section of my phone. I find this to be a faster way of getting my thoughts and ideas out without the risk of losing them (thank you, cloud storage!). By now I've compiled a lot of meaningful journal entries that I love to go back and read or listen to again.

Don't Forget Music and Laughter

Have your child create playlists for different moods or actions—whether it's a study playlist, a trampoline playlist, a road trip playlist, or a playlist to help them relax or calm down.

Spend some time reviewing and approving comedians, TV shows, and YouTube videos that encourage your children to laugh. Steer kids towards content that doesn't make jokes that are racist, sexist, or homophobic, or that otherwise come at the expense of others. Encourage them to use technology for music and laughter as part of self-care.

Practise Gratitude

Role-model gratitude for your children by saying "thank you" as much as you can in your day. Be mindful of your own complaining, and try to reduce or stop it altogether. Instead, show appreciation for the little things people do that make a difference in your day. Sweat the small stuff!

I ask my kids to think of or recite three things they're grateful for every morning and evening. I encourage them to choose different things each time. This practice works better, I find, when it's tied to a daily activity, like going to bed, brushing their teeth, or before dinner. You can also use these first or final hours of the day to tell your kids how grateful you are to have them in your life, citing specific things you appreciate about them.

Nature Is Great Therapy, Especially for Kids

Humans have a primal relationship with nature; our bodies love being outdoors. The sounds, smells, and colours of nature can lift your kids' moods and focus. Natural sunlight first thing in the morning, for example, will improve not only their mood and energy levels but also their evening sleep.

We forget that nature is full of the elements—among them water, minerals, and essential oils—that heal us. My kids take warm baths with mineral salts and oils to help their bodies and minds recover after a day of sports or stress.

Stop Perfectionism!

If you see early perfectionist behaviours, intervene! Discuss the many downsides of perfectionism, including the impact of harshly evaluating yourself and others. Explain the links to anxiety, depression, and diminished achievement. Have your child colour outside the lines, wear their hair a bit messy, hand in assignments in which they took some risks. It's good to break some rules and go against conformity—within healthy boundaries, of course!

Less Multitasking, More Mindfulness

Mindfulness is a simple technique that emphasizes paying attention to the present moment in an accepting, nonjudgmental manner. When we're focused in this way our brain gets the signal that we're safe, thus making mindfulness a useful tool for decreasing anxiety and promoting happiness.

You don't need a lot of instruction, just a lot of practice! Guide children to engage in activities mindfully, one at a time. For example, I believe that how you eat is just as important as what you eat. Eating while you're stressed out and multitasking will convert all the wonderful energy in your food into fuel for the survival system. Instead, have your kids take a few deep breaths, centre themselves, look at their food, and mindfully consume their meal. This is a key practice to help move that nutritional energy from survival to growth.

There are internet extensions and apps you can install in your child's devices that will encourage them to stay on task. For example, with one of these, called The Forest, the longer you stay on an app the more the tree grows—and if you open a blacklisted site, the tree will die.

And guess what's one of the easiest ways to encourage mindfulness? Just let your kids play! We'll dig deeper into the science of play in Chapter 7, but for now it's enough to know that non-tech play is a form of mindfulness. When your child is building a sandcastle, playing an imaginary game, doing a cartwheel, or shooting hoops in a back alley, they're fully engrossed in the moment and releasing loads of endorphins. And when play develops a rhythm, as when a child is absorbed in a drawing or a teenager is skateboarding all alone, it can become meditative.

Make Character Education and Training a Priority

Given all the messaging in our culture that leads to burnout, perfectionism, external locus of control, and the attendant problems they cause, we need to make sure our children have a clear moral compass to which they can always return. Here are a few ways to help establish a strong moral compass in your family.

- **Create a family motto or a list of family values:** These could include such traits as honesty, respect, love, integrity, humility, contribution, courage, responsibility, and citizenship. Have fun doing this, and enrich the exercise by drawing from stories of your past, your ancestors, faith, or community affiliations. Our family motto is "Work hard, think positive, make the world a better place, and have fun!"

- **Pay attention to and reinforce your child's school values:** Don't gloss over this aspect of your child's school life to focus on academics or sports. Character is tied to success more than either of those. I have my children highlight areas of their report card that comment on values such as empathy, effort, kindness, and responsibility.

- **Use sports and extracurriculars to build character:** Sports provide tons of opportunity to learn respect—for coaches, teammates, and referees—as well as cooperation, courage, and humility. Discourage bragging when your children win and encourage resiliency when they lose.

6

WIRED TO CONNECT: Oxytocin and How Tech Can Help Kids Build Community as Never Before

What you seek is seeking you.

—RUMI

NOT LONG AGO I WAS visiting New Zealand to speak at a national conference of school principals. As I do most days, I got onto FaceTime with my kids, who passed the phone to my dad. He's always wanted to see New Zealand, but he's eighty-seven now, and it occurred to me that he's unlikely to get the chance.

My father, Malkiat Kang, is a math whiz. Growing up in India, he'd always wanted to teach the subject. Finally the day came when, in the late 1940s, he was to write the exam to get into teachers' college. That morning he stopped to pick up his friend, who was also sitting for the exam. The boy's father sent them off with pakoras, a deep-fried snack made from chickpeas; the two friends devoured them as they walked. But in an effort to give his son a better chance at a seat at the college, the boy's father had laced my dad's pakoras with marijuana, effectively poisoning him. Unsurprisingly, Malkiat felt terribly sick and bombed the exam.

But he picked himself up and emigrated to Victoria, B.C., where he found work on a farm. To this day his fingers are bent and crooked from labouring through the winters without gloves—a living memory of his first job in Canada. He went on to work in lumber mills and drove taxis at night to help put food on the table and raise his five kids. Malkiat eventually moved our family to Edmonton, where he put himself through night school at the University of Alberta. Almost two and a half decades on, he finally achieved his dream of becoming a teacher.

As I spoke to him from New Zealand's South Island I held my phone in the air, the lens pointed towards the Remarkables, the jagged, misty mountain range that appears in the *Lord of the Rings* trilogy. Its gnarled forests, slicked with rain, glistened an almost iridescent green. Later I showed my dad the lightning-bolt-shaped Lake Wakatipu, the aquamarine lake that's Queenstown's crown jewel, and together we listened to the beautiful chiming call of the bellbird. It felt as though we were travelling together.

My phone has become a source of relentless distraction in my life, but for those brief moments of connection, and so many others like it, it deserves my deep appreciation. That day I felt instinctively what medical science has been increasingly demonstrating for decades: that we're hardwired to connect with others. Compassion and connection are the reasons we're here. Our relationships with others are what give purpose, meaning, and joy to our lives.

My dad was at the other end of the world in Vancouver, but in that moment what I wanted more than anything else was to see him, to be with him, to show him what all the sacrifices he'd made on my behalf had allowed me to achieve. And with a smartphone I was able to do just that.

Perhaps the most interesting thing about that conversation between my dad and me was that eleven thousand kilometres separated us that day. I didn't need to be in the same room as him to feel safe, warm, and connected. That means there are plenty of healthy ways for young people to connect online. What matters, new research shows, is what type of media your children are using. Commenting on a classmate's Instagram feed is one thing. A meaningful conversation with a close friend on Skype is quite another.

LOVE IS A NEUROCHEMICAL CALLED OXYTOCIN

When my dad and I were talking that day, looking into each other's eyes and smiling back at each other, our bodies were being flooded with a hormone known as oxytocin, the hidden key to bonding. It's another happy chemical produced by the hypothalamus in the centre of the brain.

Oxytocin has been called the "love hormone," the "cuddle hormone," the "moral molecule." It's the neurotransmitter powering connection and love in your children—producing a rush of pleasure when they hug Grandma, cuddle up to a puppy, or read a loving birthday message. It helps them maintain intimate, healthy relationships and is said to be at the core of their virtues, from trust and empathy to cooperation.

Scientists first discovered this neurochemical in new moms, who experience a surging of oxytocin after birth that makes them feel more connected to their newborns. It also helps lower their blood pressure and heart rate, making them feel less stressed. When we feel connected, we're more likely to move out of survival mode; we want to help others and care for those around us. A study of rats showed that females injected with oxytocin would care for newborn rodents when they were released into their cages—newborns they would otherwise attack.

The hormone works a lot like the love potions from fairy tales, making us feel more empathetic, generous, warm, and open to connection. One of my favourite things about oxytocin is how simple it is to get your fix: all you need to do is evoke feelings of love, compassion, and connection. A hug or even just a loving thought can do the trick.

Researchers have found that when a parent smiles, hugs, or plays with their child, oxytocin levels in both parent and child rise in step. That's because love, unlike joy or happiness, is often a two-way street. It is most powerful in the shared connection between two people. When two brains interact in this way, scientists believe that they synchronize, a process thought to be supported by what are known as "mirror neurons." These are brain cells that allow us to feel what others are feeling by subconsciously "mirroring" their behaviours and emotions. Because they allow us to see, feel, and mimic others' actions and feelings, these neurons are believed to play a role in empathy and in understanding others' intentions.

And oxytocin doesn't just come from our brains. It's also released from our hearts! Thanks to groundbreaking research by organizations like the Heart Math Institute, we can now prove what ancient cultures have known all along—that the human heart is so much more than a mechanical pump. The heart contains roughly forty thousand specialized, intelligent sensory neurites, and when we feel connected to others, these neurites release neurochemicals like oxytocin directly into our bloodstream. Our heart contains cells that also synthesize and release atrial peptide.

Atrial peptide is an intriguing hormone that I'm sure we'll be hearing more about. It's now being called the "balance hormone," since it not only plays an important role in fluid and electrolyte balance but also helps regulate the blood vessels, kidneys, adrenal glands, and many regulatory centres in the brain. Increased atrial peptide inhibits the release of stress hormones, and appears to interact with the immune system. Experiments suggest that atrial peptide can even influence motivation and behaviour.

In short, our hearts, perhaps even more than our brains, impact how we feel. And knowing that the heart actually responds physically to social interaction only underlines for us the enormous power of our relationships.

WE'RE WIRED TO CONNECT

A massive and growing body of research—from the cognitive sciences, comparative animal behaviour, and evolutionary biology— supports the idea that your child, like all humans, is an innately social creature. This need is embedded in their DNA. They *crave* community. They're driven to be curious about the people around them, to share their stories, secrets, and emotions. They're hardwired to connect to others at a deep level. In fact, without these authentic social interactions, they'll suffer.

Believe it or not, your children's need for community is as fundamental as their need for food and shelter. These connections nourish them. They centre them. They make them feel that they're loved and supported, that they count. Being tightly bonded with a community of likeminded people is "central to what makes us the most successful species on earth," neurobiologist Matthew Lieberman writes in *Social: Why Our Brains Are Wired to Connect*.

"Connecting with others is what provides richness in life, makes us feel safe, and has us recognize that we're part of something greater than ourselves."

That might help explain the enduring popularity of the internet's top website, a platform built to connect us to our friends. Indeed, if it were a religion, Facebook, with its 2.3 billion adherents, would be the world's largest, ahead of Christianity (2.1 billion) and Islam (1.5 billion).

I've mentioned how life in prehistoric times was brutal, how survival depended on being accepted into a tribe. Being cast out was an effective death sentence. Your modern-day tribe comprises the people you visit, connect with regularly, and check in on. Connecting with them makes you feel happier. And when you're happier, you tend to be a lot more fun to be around. This begets a pro-social feedback loop that looks something like this:

CONNECTION AND HAPPINESS LOOP VIA OXYTOCIN

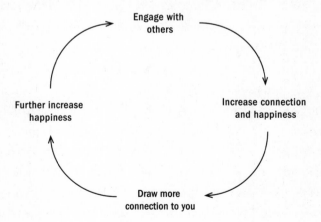

Engage with others

Increase connection and happiness

Draw more connection to you

Further increase happiness

WHY IT HURTS TO BE LEFT OUT

We're shaped by our paleolithic past, with the survival instincts we acquired to endure the harsh realities of tribal society still influencing our actions and behaviours today. That's why we yearn to fit in, why we fear rejection. We want to share good news with our tribe so that they'll continue to value us, to want to keep us within the circle. This helps explain why a cruel word from a friend or a rejection by a romantic partner can hurt so much. And if we're hurt by our loved ones in childhood, whether by abuse, neglect, or the death of a parent, it can lead to long-term health and behavioural problems.

When our ties to our community are threatened or severed, we feel what psychologists call "social pain"—and often in the heart. We see this reflected in language. The terminology of physical pain is almost universally used to express emotional pain—"She hurt my feelings," for example. The French *J'ai mal au coeur* means "My heart is aching." The Spanish *morir de pena* translates as "to die from a broken heart." German speakers, meanwhile, use *herz gebrochen* to express the feeling of having one's "heart crushed."

It's there in the language of the ancients, too. The Sumerians, one of the earliest known civilizations, had a proverb that called on the goddess of love to "pour oil on my heart that aches." Biblical references to heartache date to 1015 BC: "Insults have broken my heart and left me weak, I looked for sympathy but there was none; I found no one to comfort me" (Psalm 69:20). Rudaki, who died in 941 AD and was widely known as the father of Persian poetry, once wrote that "Thunder moans like a lover with a broken heart."

YES, SOCIAL PAIN IS REAL PAIN

Advances in neuroscience continue to demonstrate that our brains register social pain in the same place, using the same neural circuitry, as they do physical pain, yielding parallel reactions. As far as the brain is concerned, emotional and physical pain are indistinguishable. This confirms what we all know innately: that being teased, left out, or bullied can really, really hurt.

One of the most well known studies highlighting this involves a game of virtual catch that cognitive scientists call "cyberball." In a series of studies conducted in the early 2000s at UCLA's Social Cognitive Neuroscience Lab, participants were hooked up to an fMRI scanning device that registered their brain activity. While the subject of the experiment believed she was throwing the "ball" around with real people hooked up to similar screens, she was actually playing with preprogrammed avatars. After a while the avatars started throwing the ball back and forth between themselves, excluding her. That's when the woman's anterior cingulate cortex, the region involved in processing pain, lit up. She felt hurt and offended.

The experiment illustrated that something so trivial as being ignored in a simple game of catch was registered by the brain as a painful event. Further studies showed the same results, even when the person being ostracized was told they'd be paid for their isolation. This suggests that the old idiom about sticks and stones may need updating. A more accurate rendition would be *Sticks and stones may break my bones, but words can deeply wound me.*

HUMAN CONTACT IS NOW A LUXURY GOOD

While we need human contact in the same way we need food and shelter, the digital age, with its emphasis on efficiencies, self-checkouts, and digital libraries, is sharply reducing our opportunities to connect. Our modern world is increasingly built around the idea that we humans prefer the solitary life and can thrive on our own. Our economy has realigned to meet our desire to queue up a movie on Netflix and order a meal from Uber Eats without ever leaving home. But this is also realigning the way kids are interacting with the world around them.

Some are choosing to check out entirely. In Chapter 3, I mentioned Japan's *hikikomori*, young people who've sequestered themselves in their rooms, spending their time online. Closer to home, I recently started treating a teenage boy whose parents were concerned that his increasing isolation was affecting his mental health. "I really don't know why my parents brought me here," Andreas told me the first time we met. "I like being by myself. I like staying up late all alone. I chat with people online when I'm gaming. I don't need anyone else in my life. There is nothing wrong with me." Who was right?

It's true that the degree of social contact a person typically has varies widely. As the mother of both a quiet, thoughtful, more introverted child and an extrovert who speaks in a booming voice and loves telling endless stories, I see this dynamic in my own family. But was Andreas correct? Are some children perfectly all right being alone? Is love and belonging a convenience that we can live without?

Andreas claimed he didn't need people in his life, and he might indeed learn to soothe himself as best he can. But the emotional circuitry of his brain, which requires closeness and connection, will suffer grievously. For a social species like ours, being on the outskirts of society is not only sad; it can be dangerous. Extensive research has shown that monkeys raised in isolation will develop severe social deficits and reclusive tendencies, huddling in the corners of their cages, rocking mechanically, self-mutilating. When you try to house them with other monkeys, they won't learn to play or interact with the others. They become fearful, impulsive, aggressive. Their sex drive disappears. When the American psychologist Harry Harlow deprived infant rhesus macaque monkeys of social contact for a year, they were socially "obliterated," he observed, "incapable of interaction of any kind."

We don't run experiments like this on humans for obvious reasons, but researchers observed similarly devastating reactions in children rescued from impoverished Romanian orphanages in the 1990s, a time when the then Communist country outlawed abortion. Many of these children—who were left malnourished and unattended in their cribs, receiving just five or six minutes of care every day—grew up with severe social, cognitive, and behavioural issues. They had poor impulse control, low academic achievement, problems in coping and regulating emotions, low self-esteem, and pathological behaviours, including tics, tantrums, stealing, and self-punishment. Early social deprivation, scientists are beginning to understand, can alter a person's brain and behaviour. In some cases the effects of neglect will never be reversed.

Some of the best-known research into the effects of isolation was conducted in the 1990s by psychiatrist Stuart Grassian, who interviewed hundreds of prisoners spending prolonged periods in solitary confinement. Roughly one-third were "actively psychotic and/or acutely suicidal," Grassian found; he also observed hallucinations, extreme paranoia, impulsiveness, self-harm, and hypersensitivity.

Research conducted over a decade at the University of Chicago showed that socially isolated people are more irritable, more aggressive, more depressed, more sleep-deprived, more self-centred, and more likely to see unfamiliar people in a bad light. Isolated people become hypervigilant about scorn and tend to think others are being hostile—a vicious cycle.

What, I sometimes wonder, is happening in the brains of infants who are nursed by a mother holding a phone in one hand? Or in the minds of toddlers trying to play with their laptop-immersed dad? Or the teens who hardly ever seem to look up from their screens anymore? Are they missing the crucial social dance that occurs between parent and child, the opportunity to connect and bond with the people right in front of them?

THE HIGH PRICE OF LONELINESS

Your children will, unfortunately, feel loneliness at some point in their lives. The awful ache arises when their need for social connections isn't met. They might feel lonely in a crowded city, among friends and their closest family. But if this loneliness becomes persistent, it can become chronic—and pose significant risks to their health and well-being.

I don't see many elderly patients anymore, but I'll never forget one from my medical training years ago. Death was coming swiftly for her, and she knew it. Doctors had given her two weeks to live at the outside. When I gently inquired about whom she might wish to see in her final days, she told me there was no one. She had no immediate family in the city: no partner, no children. There were no close friends. There was a cousin on the opposite coast, but it had been years since they'd been in touch. Her isolation gutted me—and left me wondering whether it had played any role in her premature death from cancer.

The science would say yes. And I'm increasingly encountering teens and young adults much like her: isolated, lonely, lacking even a single close companion. The data reflects what I'm seeing in my own practice:

- Thirty years ago, when Americans were asked how many confidants they had in their lives, the most common answer was three. Today, the most common answer is zero.
- The problem is most extreme in the industrialized world, where one in three people report feeling lonely.
- Fifty percent of Canadians say they "often feel alone."
- Fifty percent of Americans say they "lack companionship or meaningful relationships."
- In a recent survey conducted in the U.K., 60 percent of respondents listed their *pet* as their closest companion.
- In Japan, there are more than a half-million people under forty who haven't left their homes or interacted with anyone for at least six months.

Loneliness not only feels awful; it can also make you depressed. It can make it hard to sleep, and it can even cause your premature death. We are a social species, and not having a social support system is a source of chronic stress for our bodies:

- Loneliness may be worse for longevity than smoking, air pollution, or obesity.
- Chronic loneliness has also been linked with an increased risk of developing or dying from everything from heart disease to dementia.

- A recent review of 148 studies concluded that being lonely increased a woman's risk of dying by 49 percent and a man's by 50 percent. And research has shown that socially isolated kids have significantly poorer health outcomes even twenty years later.
- Young people aged sixteen to twenty-four report feeling lonely more often than older age groups. For this age group, loneliness and social isolation are major precipitants of suicide.

Loneliness and suicide are complex. Not every young person feeling lonely will be suicidal, nor does loneliness always play a role in a young person's decision to attempt to end their lives. But we know that there's a link between suicide and loneliness, and that reducing loneliness can be key to reducing the risk of suicide. Every young person needs to know that it's okay to ask for help, and that someone will listen.

In summarizing his experience as a doctor, former U.S. surgeon general Vivek Murthy said that the most common pathology he saw in his time as the nation's top doctor was "not heart disease or diabetes; it was loneliness." Indeed, loneliness has been blamed for helping fuel everything from the opioid crisis and Brexit to the election of U.S. president Donald Trump and mass killings. The young man accused of killing twenty-two people at a Texas Walmart in 2019 was described by the *L.A. Times* as an "extreme loner." The same descriptor was applied to Anders Breivik, who killed seventy-seven people in Norway in 2011; the so-called Unabomber, Ted Kaczynski; and Seung-Hui Cho, who killed thirty-two people at Virginia Polytechnic Institute and State University in 2007.

Loneliness has become such a problem in Britain that in 2018 the government appointed a "minister for loneliness" to try to address it. British firefighters have been trained to inspect homes for signs of social isolation. Postal workers are being dispatched on door-knocking campaigns to check in on elderly residents, all part of the country's "Campaign to End Loneliness." And across the U.K. some three hundred "Men's Sheds" have opened—communal workshops aimed at bringing older men and retirees together to talk as they tinker with anything from bicycles to bookshelves.

Despite its prevalence, especially in the industrialized world, people tend to shy away from talking about loneliness. We consider it a sad and shameful condition, "the psychological equivalent to being a loser in life, or a weak person," John Cacioppo, who spent decades studying loneliness, said in a TEDx Talk. Denying loneliness, he told his audience, makes no more sense than denying you feel thirst or hunger.

ARE ONLINE CONNECTIONS GOOD CONNECTIONS?

The promise of the internet has always been contact, the key ingredient of social health. Social media messaging includes chatter about bringing the world "closer together" (Facebook's mission statement). In its infancy, the internet seemed to offer an antidote to loneliness by helping people develop virtual belonging, no matter how shy or isolated they might be. These relationships can be a "life raft for those who have nothing else," psychiatrist Allen Frances told Canada's *National Post* newspaper in 2019. But, he added, "they can also be an anchor that drags people into even more isolation."

Consider what you've observed in your own kids. Think of the last time your daughter was sitting on the couch with her friends, all of them texting or Snapping away. There was no face-to-face contact. She wasn't giggling or hugging or high fiving with her pals; she wasn't doing any of the things that we know would flood her system with oxytocin, making her feel loved and connected. If your daughter is like a lot of kids I know, she's communicating incessantly but rarely having a real conversation. Her hangouts are happening on group texts.

And yet there are also plenty of healthy ways for young people to connect online. What matters, new research shows, is what *types* of media they're using. In a 2016 study, a team of researchers at Lafayette College in Easton, Pennsylvania, found that toddlers were able to learn to clap and imitate when they were paired with a researcher via FaceTime. Crucially, though, when the calls were prerecorded and the child could neither see nor hear their partner, they *didn't* learn. This suggests that, even when our relationships are mediated by tech, we need to continue to experience their most human aspects in order to experience deep and meaningful connections.

You've probably noticed this in your own life. Have you ever gone on FaceTime and felt really excited to see someone, whether it's your best friend's new baby or your younger brother whom you haven't visited in a long time? I feel very fortunate to be able to get on the road and talk to parents about the ups and downs of raising kids. But when I'm out for a long stretch I miss my own kids! So I've established a routine to try to make things easier for all of us. Whenever I arrive at a new hotel I try to get on FaceTime to show my kids my room for the night and tell them about whatever city or country I happen to find myself in. As soon as I see their smiling faces in real time, I feel a rush of pleasure. I start to relax and feel a sense of calm come over me. At times these conversations can feel even more meaningful than some of the ones we have at home when I'm rushing to get them to bed! Clearly, video chat is facilitating healthy connections.

A study published in 2018 looked at whether Skype could help older people beat the blues. The results of the study—led by Alan Teo, a professor of psychiatry at the Oregon Health and Science University—were stunning: those who used video chat were half as likely to be depressed at a two-year follow-up than those who used email, social media, and text messaging.

These studies show that genuine online connections are possible via live video, even among the very old and the very young. So, again, whether your kids are connecting online depends on how they're actually going about it.

A lot of people in my field disdain television and video games and counsel parents to ban them. But I tend to think they can offer meaningful ways to connect. I can see the camaraderie and hear the laughter of my sons' squads when they play video games, and the delight in my daughter's face when her cousin sends her a special, personalized video. And every Thanksgiving my family gathers around the TV with our phones in hand to watch CNN's "Everyday Heroes" special. The two-hour event, hosted by broadcaster Anderson Cooper, recognizes people who go to extraordinary lengths to help others. It's interactive, allowing my family to learn, to be part of the process by voting for their favourite choice, and to be inspired along the way.

READING, WRITING, 'RITHMETIC . . . RELATIONSHIPS?
I try to tell parents that kids don't need four hundred online friends. Nor do parents need to arrange playdates with their kids' friends from soccer, from school, from gymnastics, from camp.

That's unrealistic and unnecessary. All kids really need are one or two close friends and a greater sense of community. The quality of the two or three relationships they do have is what really matters. Indeed, as a remarkable 2010 study conducted at Montreal's Concordia University showed, a single friend is enough to ward off depression in anxious, withdrawn children.

Kids, just like parents, go through ups and downs. Those who are shy and awkward tend to have a harder time fitting in—and for these kids, the angst typical of adolescence can spiral out of control. But the Concordia study showed that, among preteens, a good friend is enough to arrest the pull towards depression. The child's friend seemed to at once protect them from depression and bestow them with resilience. Dr. William Bukowski, a professor of psychology and the study's lead author, believes that parents should be treating friendship as the fourth R. As he puts it, "After 'reading, writing, and 'rithmetic,' it should be 'relationships.'"

We parents often become laser-focused on academic achievement. (And I'm the first to admit that I'm sometimes guilty of this!) But when we do, we can overlook a great way to maintain emotional health, particularly through the rocky adolescent years. A key role for all parents is to help our children develop meaningful, positive connections. When they're young we can help arrange playdates and sleepovers and group hikes or park visits. There comes a time, though, when they no longer need us for this, and we have to take a step back from their social lives. But that doesn't mean we have to pull out completely. We can encourage uplifting friendships. We can talk about how to develop and negotiate healthy relationships and how important our own friends have been to us.

Remember, socializing may be fun, but it's not the same as social bonding. And commenting on someone's social media feed is definitely not social bonding.

THE END OF EMPATHY?

A friend recently told me about something she'd noticed when she was pregnant and riding the bus to and from work each day. Even in her eighth month—visibly pregnant and obviously uncomfortable— no one would give up their seat for her the way they had just seven years earlier, when she'd been pregnant the first time. She wondered if this reflected a societal change: *Are people becoming more selfish? Less empathetic? Have they become so engrossed in their phones and social media that they've stopped noticing—or even caring—about the discomfort and distress of those around them?*

My friend isn't the only one who believes society is becoming increasingly cruel, callous, and disconnected:

- Fifty-one percent of Britons said empathy has noticeably declined, according to a 2018 YouGov survey.
- Empathy in university students is down by 40 percent since 1980, with an especially steep drop in the last ten years, according to an extensive 2010 study by the University of Michigan that examined twenty years of data on university students' self-reported empathy.
- Levels of narcissism among university-aged youth have meanwhile risen by 58 percent, the same study showed.

CARSON'S STORY

When I read about the death of a fourteen-year-old boy named Carson Crimeni in August 2019, I asked myself the same questions as my friend did. Carson, who'd recently finished grade nine, his first year of high school, died in a Langley, B.C., park from a drug overdose while he was out with a group of older kids. The death of a child is always tragic. But the facts of this case were deeply disturbing.

Carson, who had a severe form of ADHD, had been relentlessly bullied in school, and so the invitation to hang out with a group of much older teens was a rare thrill. When he was intoxicated and in distress, the teens he was with gave him drugs, mocked him, and filmed him over several hours. Not one of the young people with him that night thought to help Carson or call police. Instead they made him a meme, posting his ordeal to Snapchat and Instagram, pairing photos and short videos with witty taglines.

In one video taken that night, captioned "12-year-old tweaking on molly," Carson appears heavily intoxicated, allegedly on MDMA, a party drug also known as ecstasy. He's sweating through his grey hoodie, swaying to music while a group of young men howl and catcall him. This carries on over several hours that night, even as the boy is overheating and losing the ability to speak. Teens burst into laughter when Carson can't seem to recall his name. At that point he curls inward, hugging himself. He looks terrified. In the final photo taken that night, a teen leans towards the ambulance attending to the boy in the background. "Carson almost died lol" the caption reads. Within minutes, Carson was in fact dead.

For Gen Z youth, who spend around nine hours online every day, memes—captioned images or videos meant to be funny or sarcastic—have become one of the most popular ways to communicate. But in a world where comments and followers have become measures of popularity and an "all-about-the-likes" sense of values dominates, the bar for outrageous behaviour is constantly being raised. Carson's aunt, Diane Crimeni, told *The Globe and Mail* that she worries that today's youth, who are viewing everything through a screen, have trouble discerning reality: "To them, nothing seems real. . . . How many kids sat at home watching Carson dying in front of their eyes but did nothing?" Diane believes that if someone had instilled empathy, whether in the bystanders or in the kids who targeted Carson, her nephew might still be alive today.

Sympathy Versus Empathy

Sympathy and empathy are commonly confused traits. And although people often use the two words interchangeably, they're related but different feelings.

Sympathy is the ability to express sorrow, compassion, or pity for someone's situation, and to sit *with* their experience. It boils down to an ability to notice and be moved by the distress of another.

Empathy, according to psychologist Alfred Adler, is "seeing with the eyes of another, listening with the ears of another, and feeling with the heart of another." It boils down to the ability to understand what someone else is going through, to sit *within* their experience.

Raising Empaths

Most kids can feel sympathy, but not all kids can feel empathy. Although there may be some genetic underpinnings, it's also a learned trait that needs to be nurtured and encouraged. Our kids develop it primarily through face-to-face interactions—when they're best able to see the full human reality of the person standing in front of them.

Empathetic kids, who have the ability to walk in another person's shoes, are the ones who stand up to bullies. They're the ones who take action and make the world a better place for us all. They tend to go on to become well-adjusted adults who treat others with respect, understanding, and compassion. Conversely, a lack of empathy in children is associated with bullying, cheating, weak moral reasoning, and such mental health issues as anxiety and depression. It can be hard for kids lacking empathy to build meaningful relationships. Their behaviour can be viewed as hurtful when they disregard the thoughts and feelings of others.

But empathy is learned best if it's experienced. And as parents, we provide the first opportunities for our children to feel empathy's powerful effects.

The reasons cited for declines in empathy include an increase in screen time and social media use, the rise of hypercompetitive parenting and celebrity culture, a focus on standardized testing in schools, and a decrease in playtime. In a 2014 study by the University of California at Los Angeles, sixth graders who went five days without so much as glancing at a screen or using any tech devices were substantially better at reading facial cues and identifying emotions than their peers, who continued to spend several hours a day on their devices. "It's very hard to be empathetic and feel for another human being if you can't read another person's emotions," explains psychologist Michelle Borba. You don't learn emotional literacy with emojis, memes, and tweets. According to Stanford neuroscientist Jamil Zaki, too often these days, "our interactions with one another are online, anonymous and tribal—barren soil for empathy."

A 2017 study by New York University psychologist William Brady and his team analyzed some five hundred thousand tweets on polarizing topics, including gun control, same-sex marriage, and climate change, trying to determine why some went viral and others fell flat. Brady found that the more "moral emotion"—the more outrage—a tweet contained, the more it was retweeted. What this means is that your child's social media feed isn't simply mirroring an angry world back at him; it's helping to create one.

The thing is, not all screen time results in kids losing the ability to understand and share in the feelings of others. We know from experience that social media is also facilitating countless collaborations and helping to raise awareness and millions of dollars for worthy causes. A GoFundMe campaign raised more than $15 million for the Humboldt Broncos players and families after the hockey team's bus crashed on a highway in Saskatchewan in 2018. A similar campaign raised more than $40,000 for Carson Crimeni's family in the wake of the teen's death. As we learned in this chapter, technology isn't necessarily robbing your child of empathy. It can also help foster the trait in your children, just as the right use of technology can help your kids develop meaningful, positive connections with others.

REMEMBER . . .

- Your children, like all humans, are innately social creatures. It's embedded in their DNA.
- They need both an *individual* and a *group* identity. Children crave community and group acceptance. They yearn to fit in. They fear rejection.
- They're driven by deep motivations to stay connected to their friends and family, to be curious about the people around them, to share stories, secrets, and emotions.
- The need to connect is as fundamental as your child's need for food and shelter.
- Oxytocin, the so-called "cuddle hormone," is the neurochemical powering love, connection, and trust. It floods your kids' systems, producing a rush of pleasure when they hug Grandma, play with a puppy, or read a special birthday message.
- Loneliness may be worse for your kids' longevity than smoking, air pollution, or obesity.
- Empathy can be taught and developed.
- A fundamental role for parents and educators is to guide children towards empathy and healthy social relationships.
- Standard psychological tests are showing a steep decline in empathy in the smartphone generation, and screen time is being fingered for part of the blame.
- Not all screen time is causing kids to lose the ability to understand and share the feelings of others. Video communication is better, since humans need to see each other's faces.

SOLUTIONS

In this chapter we learned that your children are social creatures; when they experience bonding and love they feel safe, empowered, and motivated through the release of oxytocin. For a social species like ours isolation and loneliness can be dangerous, yet the digital age is restricting our opportunities to connect. It's therefore crucially important to help your children enhance meaningful connections with the people in their lives.

In the pages ahead I'll provide you with ways to help your children establish healthy relationships, avoid dangerous ones, and assert themselves within friendships and relationships with their peers. These practices will help build the future-ready CQ (Consciousness Quotient) skills of communication, collaboration, and contribution. I'll also explore how parents can help prevent cyberbullying and sexting, two common behaviours among young people that compromise healthy bonding and community.

KEY STRATEGIES

DON'T

- Assume digital connection is meaningful connection
- Ignore the issue of loneliness in children and teens
- Keep your child so busy that they have no time to build connections
- Look at your phone when you're talking to your child

DO

- Guide your child to a healthy relationship with themselves
- Teach your child how to find and be a good friend
- Monitor and develop empathy
- Teach, model, and practise healthy assertiveness
- Explain the difference between conflicts, mean behaviour, and bullying

AVOID . . .

Any type of negative online connection: scammers, predators, online arguments, cyberbullying, mean friends, unhealthy relationships, and media that induces FOMO or comparisons

LIMIT AND MONITOR . . .

Superficial, meaningless connections, such as Snapchat streaks or memes

ENCOURAGE . . .

Tech that fosters meaningful connections. Examples include video communication, positive emails, webinars, text messaging, and some social media.

HOW TO BUILD HEALTHY RELATIONSHIPS

Relationship skills, just like reading and math skills, are developed one step at a time. Your children can't establish healthy relationships with others unless they have a healthy relationship with themselves. I often ask my patients: *How will anyone love you if you don't love yourself? How are you going to connect with someone if you can't connect with yourself?* I call this their "inner-personal relationship." It's arguably the most important relationship in life.

Your children will develop self-confidence and self-trust when they spend time alone and get to know themselves. Here are a few ways you can help:

- Guide your child towards self-compassion. Teach them to forgive themselves for mistakes. Remind them that they're children, and that mistakes are part of growing up. Instead of regret and self-criticism, have them figure out the lessons learned from the mistake and what they'd do differently next time.

- Guide them to evaluate and build on the aspects of their personality that serve them and work to change those that don't. For example, if they tend to blow up at people and regret it later, explain that they've developed this habit and that, with training over time, they can develop other ways to communicate.

- Celebrate their efforts and small wins towards self-care and positive change. Praise efforts towards and demonstrations of self-compassion, such as distancing themselves from unhealthy friendships despite peer pressure, or saying no to getting back on the field after an injury in a sports game.

HOW TO FIND AND BE A GOOD FRIEND

It's important that children recognize the difference between healthy and unhealthy friendships. When I teach kids to spot the difference, I go back to the three animal metaphors: the *dolphin*, *the shark*, and *the jellyfish* (pages 32–4). Just like the parenting relationship, the dolphin is the ideal type of friend. The shark and jellyfish are less than ideal. Use these metaphors to help tweens and teens better understand and evaluate their relationships with their classmates, friends, and romantic partners, and to help them make choices about the kinds of people they want to have in their lives.

Dolphin friends are firm and flexible, just like the body of the marine mammal. They . . .

- Have strong values, such as honesty, respect, integrity, and compassion
- Are flexible with the little things in life—which restaurant to eat at, which game to play
- Use communication and collaboration as essential relationship tools
- View compromise as healthy as long as it doesn't mean compromising any of their core values
- Are curious—not judgmental—about differences in opinion and in people
- Adapt easily to life's ups and downs; if a friend can't make their birthday party, they understand
- Strive to contribute, and to help others
- Value, participate in, and help build the community around them

Jellyfish friends are spineless and free floating, like the marine invertebrates. They . . .

- Don't voice their opinions and beliefs
- Are overly permissive and let other people walk all over them
- Don't stand up for themselves
- Are willing to compromise their values
- Tend to avoid conflict in the short term, which over time leads to becoming a people pleaser, a follower, or even being bullied

Shark friends are aggressive and out for themselves, like the solitary ocean fish. They . . .

- Are overbearing by being too pushy or micromanaging
- Are self-centred
- Are judgmental
- Throw their weight around in negotiations
- May get what they want in the short term, but create unhealthy relationship patterns

At different times and depending on the issue and/or the relationship, your children will be jellyfish, sharks, or dolphins. Keep in mind, though, that our external behaviours most often reflect what's happening internally. So guide your child towards seeking out those friends who are able to self-regulate and who understand stress management and the importance of self-care. They're the ones less likely to become sharks or jellyfish; these are the dolphins you want to bring into your pod.

The Dolphin Assertiveness Technique

Even the best friendships can have tensions! So it's important to teach children how to engage in healthy communication and positive assertiveness that will solidify their friendships. Just like the body of a dolphin, this technique is based on being firm and flexible in your communication with others. For example, if your child's friend is being a shark about playing video games, you might encourage them to respond in the following way:

Firm: "No thanks, I don't want to play video games right now."

Flexible: "We could play basketball or jump on the trampoline? We can also plan to play video games another time."

The Sandwich Method of Communication

You can take the dolphin assertiveness technique one step further by sandwiching a firm, assertive statement (which could be perceived as criticism) between two positive statements. This is a sensitive communication strategy that will encourage your child to be clear and direct while maintaining a positive tone.

For example, if your child is unhappy about a photo of her posted to social media, she could address it this way:

Positive statement: Tara, thanks so much for inviting me to the party last night. It was a lot of fun!

Assertive statement: I noticed a photo of me taken at the party on social media that made me uncomfortable. Could you please take it down?

Positive statement: I can't wait until we get together again!

HOW DO I TEACH EMPATHY?

We can't assume that children will just develop the powerful skill of empathy—especially in our fast-paced, technologically driven world. So it's essential that parents be intentional about guiding their children towards empathy. Here are some tips:

- Teach kids to always make eye contact with others.
- Expose them to lots of different people.
- Talk about bullying incidents.
- After a conflict, discuss what everyone was feeling.
- Model respect for those who seem different.

GUIDE CHILDREN TOWARDS CONTRIBUTION

Humans are social beings, hardwired to contribute and to feel rewarded by it. The highest form of human motivation is known as "mission" or "purpose"—fuelled as it is by our connection to the world and our desire to positively contribute to it. And when we do so, we're rewarded with a "helper's high" of dopamine.

Contribution can be embedded in every activity, not just volunteer work. When a child performs well in school, in sports, or in a school play, remind them that their efforts positively impacted others, whether through direct contribution or the role modelling of effort, resilience, and perseverance. Guiding children towards forging a strong connection to their family, friends, community, and the planet, and using that connection to drive them, will lead to lifelong motivation!

One way to build strong connections is to encourage small acts of kindness in real life and online:

- Guide children towards "cyberbacking." Practise saying something kind or having a friend's back online—especially if they see something cruel being said about them.
- Help them get involved in online community-building activities—anything from GoFundMe pages for local causes to disaster relief for large international issues. Remember, involvement doesn't always have to include donating money. Simply forwarding an email to friends, liking, or leaving a positive comment are all powerful ways to connect.
- Encourage them to send kind text messages, cute emojis, or brief voice memos to friends and family who may need a pick-me-up—or just to spread some love around!
- Encourage your child to accept attention in the form of "likes" and friend or follow requests in a positive way. It's important for them to learn to be comfortable receiving praise, and to reciprocate kind behaviour. Have them practise saying a simple "Thank you for the compliment, it means a lot to me." (This is very different from *needing* praise. The habit of looking for praise in order to feel good about themselves may initially provide some motivation, but it won't last, and can ultimately lead to a destructive cycle of insecurity.) Encouraging children in this way will guide them towards receiving "likes" not as ego inflaters but as inspiration to power further contribution.

HOW TO PREVENT CYBERBULLYING

Even if your child is working on developing healthy communication skills and empathy, there's a good chance they might encounter peers that are more aggressive and shark-like in their behaviour.

Cyberbullying is characterized by the repetitive use of smartphones and apps to harm someone by making them angry, sad, or scared. This could involve sending hurtful messages or posting embarrassing photos on social media.

Some 87 percent of teens have witnessed this type of bullying. Therefore, make it a practice to ask your child about cyberbullying, mean behaviour, and other conflicts they encounter while online, and encourage them to come to you when they see something that makes them uncomfortable. And it's not a conversation to have just once or twice. You need to keep talking to your children about it in increasingly complex ways as they get older. You can approach the subject in a variety of ways:

- Refer to stories or news you may have heard or read about.
- Ask open-ended questions. *Why do you think cyberbullying can hurt? Have you ever seen someone get bullied this way?*
- Remind them that you're asking because you care about their well-being. Reassure them that you won't automatically freak out and confront other students or parents, take their devices away, or send them to another school.
- Talk about what they can do if they're ever bullied in this way.

What to Do if Your Child Is Being Cyberbullied

- Reassure your child that they're safe, supported, and loved despite what they may have seen or heard.
- Tell them that the situation can be managed, and that it'll be over in time.
- Remind them that telling an adult isn't tattling—it's standing up for yourself. It will also help the bully in the long run.
- Have them take a break from the device, whether it's a mobile phone or a laptop. Advise them not to look for disturbing content, especially when they're alone. If they insist on knowing what's being said about them, look it up yourself or ask a trusted third party to look at it for them.
- Encourage them to spend some time with real friends offline. This will help reduce the intensity of the experience and remind your child that they have good friends they can trust.
- Consider contacting the school or police. Don't hesitate if there's any content that may constitute hate speech or child pornography.
- Whether your child has been bullied or your child is the bully, consider reaching out to the other parents involved.
- If they've posted something they regret, help them take down the content and make amends for any harm they may have caused.
- Teach them not to respond in the heat of the moment. They may say something they could later regret.
- Teach them not to engage with the bully in real life until they've discussed the situation with a responsible adult. Bullies are looking for a reaction, so don't provide one.

- Block the phone number, accounts, and emails of anyone sending offensive content.
- If necessary to prove bullying allegations, consider collecting evidence—take screenshots. Save and print out bullying messages for proof, in case you need it.

SEXTING

Sexting is still a relatively new and complex topic that we're understanding more about—and that continues to evolve. On the one hand, some exploration of sexuality and romantic relationships is a normal part of development in the teenage years. On the other hand, sexting can become unhealthy and toxic.

Sexting involves sharing intimate content, images, or videos with another person, whether via text, private messages on social networks, or apps. Often, sexting occurs between young people who are dating or considering dating, but it can also take place between friends or groups. The content could be anything from sexually driven text messages to partial or full nude photos, videos, or pornography.

As a parent, you need to understand the pressures. In a 2015 Michigan State University study, 24 percent of the teens said they'd been sexually harassed by people they considered their friends. A lot of teens who share intimate content feel shame or regret afterwards. Research has also found that "people afraid of looking bad in a partner's eyes sexted more than people emotionally secure in their relationship."

So What Should Parents Do?

- Make sure that sexting is part of your birds-and-the-bees talk.
- Don't wait for an incident to occur before talking to your child about healthy sexuality and relationships. Ask your child, "Have you heard of sexting?" They may know more than you! This will also help make sure that the conversations are age appropriate.
- Answer their questions about sexting truthfully, but there's no need to give them too much information. This will require multiple conversations over time in different ways as your child grows.
- Make sure they understand that underage sexting may be considered a crime in many jurisdictions.
- Advise them to immediately delete any sexting images that are sent to them.
- Tell them to never ask for sexually explicit photos or images from someone.
- Remind teens that once something is seen it can't be unseen, and that once something is sent it can't be retrieved. A good wake-up call is to ask them how they'd feel if their grandparents, teachers, coaches, or cousins saw the image.
- Explain that although they may feel intense pressure to send or ask for a photo, this can have harmful long-term consequences and is best avoided.

7

WIRED TO CREATE: Serotonin and How to Help Your Child Own Their Future

Life is really simple, but we insist on making it complicated.

—CONFUCIUS

THERE'S NOTHING TYPICAL about Lilly Singh. In the fall of 2019, the thirty-one-year-old comedian debuted *A Little Late with Lilly Singh* on NBC. She hadn't come up through film or TV; instead, she'd built her name and fortune by writing, directing, and starring in YouTube videos shot from her bedroom. Collectively, they've had more than one billion views.

Singh grew up in suburban Toronto, worshipping Dwayne "The Rock" Johnson and dreaming of a career in hip hop, but her hardworking parents pushed her towards more traditional pursuits. Then, when she was twenty-two and studying psychology at Toronto's York University, she began struggling with severe depression: "I was going through the motions of life and doing what my family wanted me to do."

Finding herself with a lot of free time on her hands, she started watching funny YouTube videos to cheer herself up. One day, Singh spontaneously decided to post something herself—a spoken word poem she later took down because it was "so crazy." Still, the poem got seventy views, which at the time felt to her like fame: "It boggled my mind. How did these people find this video?" she told the *Hollywood Reporter*. "Who were they and why were they watching it?" More importantly, it ignited a passion in Singh. "After so many lectures in school, here was this project where I could do what I loved," she told *New York* magazine in 2019.

That first video led to a second, then a third. As she grew more comfortable in front of the Canon T3i DSLR camera she'd bought on sale—and taught herself more about lighting, angles, and video editing—she set about establishing her brand, a kind of wacky, observational comedy focusing on teen culture and her South Asian heritage. Before long she was posting twice weekly under the persona Superwoman. By 2017, *Forbes* pegged Singh as the highest-paid woman on YouTube and the platform's third-highest earner overall.

Singh, who likes loud colours and backwards trucker hats, embodies YouTube's DIY ethos. In 2019 she made TV history by taking over Carson Daly's slot on NBC. And whereas Daly had taken the traditional route to TV fame, first as a radio DJ, then as a VJ on MTV, Singh used digital tools to create a new path, teaching herself everything from camerawork to comedic timing.

THE CREATIVE CHILD

Your children are wired for the kind of creativity that Singh used as a stepping stone to global fame. After all, kids are born creators. It's in their DNA. Your children are never more authentic and truer to themselves than when they're creating something.

There's no concrete definition of the term "creativity," which has always been a somewhat fuzzy concept. But most agree that it's the power to come up with something new, whether it's a novel idea or design, a link between ideas, or a solution to a problem. The word "creative" comes from the Latin *creare*, meaning to bring forth, to beget. Creativity isn't limited to works of genius. Nor is it limited to original prodigies. It resides in every one of us.

Enlightenment thinkers like Thomas Hobbes and John Locke saw in human imagination and creativity the path to human progress. Indeed, creativity has always been the great driver of evolution and growth. It's an essential component of what makes us human. We alone can imagine something and then go out and make it real, whether it's a painting of a mastodon on a cave wall, a cure for a disease, or a virtual reality treadmill. This innately human potential is what differentiates *Homo sapiens*—Latin for "wise man"—from our hominid ancestors.

I tend to think of the human mind as a fingerprint: no two children have the same thought patterns and brain anatomy. Each is entirely unique, the result of genetic factors and their life experiences. Our children must learn to develop their identity, passions, and talents by tapping into the vast reservoirs of creative potential that exist within each of them. Their autonomy, mastery, and purpose can't be imposed from the outside by anyone, not even parents. This chapter explores the ways technology can help children discover their individual passions, feed their creativity, and find their true purpose and calling in life.

THIS IS YOUR BRAIN ON SEROTONIN

Each of us longs to feel significant. None of us wants to die without leaving a legacy, an impact, some sign of our existence. Our brains evolved to seek respect and esteem from others. That's why it feels good when you're admired or put in charge of something. The hidden key to this behaviour is serotonin—a neurochemical that produces feelings of safety, contentment, and confidence. It also bolsters self-esteem, increases feelings of creativity and worthiness, and helps keep anxiety at bay.

Think back to a moment when you felt proud of yourself. Perhaps you achieved an important personal goal or received recognition from your colleagues. The confidence and strength you felt came from a buildup of serotonin in your brain. This neurochemical helps your children's creative minds thrive. They release it when using apps or websites or playing games that expand their creativity or awareness of the world. When they learn, imagine, collaborate, create, or feed their passions, whether by writing, painting, or playing music, it stimulates cognitive and physiological processes that feed and expand their creative capacities. This increases their serotonin levels, leading them to feel happy, confident, and content. Other powerful stimulators of serotonin release include sunlight, exercise, and social connection.

Decreased levels of serotonin can lead to children feeling down, getting easily annoyed, or being unable to control their impulses. Serotonin dysfunction, in fact, is thought to lead to anxiety and depression. In experiments with bioengineered mice, researchers found that those lacking serotonin early in life, when their brains were rapidly developing, displayed anxious behaviour as adults. Studies have shown that stress crushes creativity. Primates under stress will not pursue new territories or mates. When stressed, we humans also tend to cling to the familiar.

Medications that are used to combat anxiety and depression—among them Prozac (fluoxetine), Celexa (citalopram), and Zoloft (sertraline)—work on the serotonin system. Meds like these are in a class of drugs called selective serotonin reuptake inhibitors (SSRIs). They act by limiting the neurotransmitter's reabsorption, allowing it to linger longer in the brain.

SIX WAYS TECH IS BOOSTING CREATIVITY

Humans evolved to create—and tech is increasingly allowing kids to dream bigger than ever before. It lets them see the world differently, access information from anywhere they wish, and find and develop new passions, concepts, and ideas. Here are six ways tech can help enhance creativity in your children:

1. **Information:** This may be the single most important ingredient for creativity. If for nothing else, the internet exists to share information. At this point, kids can access information on just about any subject they can think of.

2. **Efficiency:** Tech has sped up the creative process. Consider writing. Whether it's fiction or non-fiction, computers and word processors have made the writing and editing process much faster and easier. A few notable holdouts remain—authors Neil Gaiman, Joyce Carol Oates, and Stephen King are said to still prefer writing their novels longhand—but they're the exceptions!

3. **Access:** Any teenager with a cellphone can snap a picture or shoot a video. The tools needed to take beautiful photos or create a basic podcasting setup are becoming increasingly accessible to the

average person, broadening your children's access to a range of creative mediums that were once out of reach.

4. **Collaboration:** Tech has made it easier than ever to collaborate with like-minded or diverse-minded young people around the world. And when we collaborate, we exchange ideas that can lead to innovation.

5. **Online learning:** The ability to access online learning opportunities like MasterClass gives your kids the chance to learn the basic skills involved in a number of creative fields, including writing, reporting, screenwriting, directing, acting, and cooking.

6. **New tools:** 3D printing, storytelling, and video creation tools give kids the chance to explore new things and to express themselves in various ways and in various media.

THE WONDERS OF ASSISTIVE TECH

Just as YouTube provided a future for Lilly Singh in a way her parents couldn't have imagined, tech provided a better future for my son Joesh. When he was nine, Joesh was diagnosed with dysgraphia and a disorder of written expression. This means he has trouble putting thoughts to paper, and even if he could, his handwriting is pretty much illegible. He was later diagnosed with attention deficit hyperactivity disorder (ADHD); he can become distracted, impulsive, and a bit loud. He can also be forgetful and disorganized, and has trouble managing his schedule. Not long ago, Joesh would have floundered in school. Teachers and school officials would have written him off as lazy, messy, and stupid. Statistically speaking, it's doubtful he would have made it through high school—which would have severely limited his self-esteem, career options, and possibly his life happiness. But for Joesh, the world of assistive technology has opened up an entirely different future.

Because of his dysgraphia, he uses typing and a voice dictation system for homework, essays, and exams. Because of his ADHD he uses noise-cancelling headphones in class and during exams to help improve his focus, along with calendar reminders, and digital organizers to help manage his time. Without these tools, Joesh would be lost in the school system.

Today he's a confident teenager with a lovely, positive personality that draws people to him. Joesh has an amazing memory and loves obscure facts; he's quick on his feet, social, and charismatic. He's also a talented public speaker, taking part in international competitions (and once, when he was twelve, he received a standing ovation from a group of five hundred adults for a speech he delivered on racial inequality). His memory, social skills, and public speaking ability helped him recognize that although he may have a deficit in some areas, he also has talents that others don't. Public speaking has since become a passion of his. He knows his future is bright. I shudder to think what his life might have been like had he been born even a decade earlier.

By offering new mediums for learning, expression, and creativity, assistive technologies like the ones Joesh relies on are increasingly levelling the educational playing field for kids with learning differences and mental and physical health issues, including ADHD, language processing disorder, visual perceptual/visual motor disorder, autism spectrum, and dyslexia.

Perhaps the greatest pioneer in assistive tech was Stephen Hawking, the Cambridge University physicist who died in 2018 at the age of seventy-six. Diagnosed with a neuromuscular wasting disorder known as amyotrophic lateral sclerosis (ALS) or Lou Gehrig's disease when he was a twenty-one-year-old graduate student, he went on to show us the long-term potential for success these technologies provide. He also illustrated how, for those who might not otherwise have the ability, tech can open up opportunities to make significant contributions to our knowledge and culture.

Hawking became a cultural icon and one of the world's best-known science communicators, reaching global audiences with *A Brief History of Time*—a sharp, witty book on cosmology that spent a record-breaking four and a half years on the London *Times* bestseller list. He said he tried to avoid weighing the book down with scientific jargon and to write in the most accessible, matter-of-fact style he could. He wanted to give regular people the "feeling that they need not be cut off from the great intellectual and philosophical questions." Over the course of his life Hawking managed to publish dozens of scientific papers, editorials, and children's books. He also gave speeches all over the world, despite being slowly paralyzed by ALS.

When he lost the ability to talk, Hawking had a thumb switch attached to his keyboard that allowed him to compose speeches and "speak" through a voice synthesizer. Then, in the last few years of his life, when he was too weak to move his fingers, he communicated with the help of word prediction algorithms. By tensing his cheek and blinking his right eye, he was still able to control his computer.

In his lifetime, Hawking contributed more to our understanding of the early universe and the behaviour of black holes than any scientist since Albert Einstein. And if not for assistive tech, that knowledge might have stayed locked in his brain.

SCHOOL LESSONS FROM CHINA

Let's now explore the ways your children's education is helping to foster their creativity—or not.

Every three years, like clockwork, countries around the world take notice of each other's school systems. It happens when the PISA scores are released. The Programme for International Student Assessment is an international test that scores fifteen-year-olds in math, sciences, and reading. Shanghai and Hong Kong fifteen-year-olds consistently sit atop the global rankings. The "brutal truth," said the American education secretary—after the 2009 PISA results placed the U.S. twenty-fourth, well behind Shanghai and Hong Kong at number one and two, respectively—is that "we're being out-educated."

The scores signal to Western media, politicians, and policymakers that China's high test scores = educational excellence = a system worth emulating. Western governments attempt to make their schools more "Chinese" by removing recess and gym, introducing more exams, and making more rigorous demands of students. Beijing, meanwhile, is taking the country's schools in the opposite direction, *away* from rote learning, memorization, long days, and lots of homework. Sure, that system produces great test takers. But Chinese officials are well aware of its deficits.

With creative disruption continuing to drive the modern global economy, China knows that it's graduating robotized students ill-equipped for meeting its needs. And it has the data to prove it, as I learned on a visit to Shanghai's Fudan University during my book tour for *The Dolphin Parent*. This is where I met with the think tank tasked with charting a new direction for the country's school system.

Every Chinese student who wishes to attend university must write the National College Entrance Examination (NCEE), commonly known as *gaokao* exam. For the last fifty years the Chinese government has been collecting hundreds of millions of data points on the NCEE. In Shanghai, I was asked what I thought happened to those who placed atop the NCEE's ranks every year. The shocking answer: nothing at all. China's top students don't go on to write new patents, invent new technologies, or discover cures to diseases. They simply "disappear" after university.

The country's policymakers are not unaware that Jack Ma, China's best-known business magnate, not only failed the *gaokao* twice but once scored just 1 out of 120 on the math section. Ma did eventually make it into university, where he earned middling grades as an English major—before going on to found Alibaba, the world's largest e-commerce company, from his apartment in 1999.

"I told my son: You don't need to be in the top three in your class," Ma once said in a speech. "Being in the middle is fine. Only a [middle-of-the-road student] has enough free time to learn other skills." Like Ma, many of China's top tech executives were average students.

As China shifts to a system that it hopes will produce innovation-ready students, it has begun limiting the frequency and importance of exams in schools. It's also introducing policies to restrict students' workload and prohibiting schools from offering extra tutoring after school hours and during summer and winter breaks. And it's expanding education beyond traditional subjects to emphasize CQ, or Consciousness Quotient: creativity, critical thinking, communication, collaboration, and contribution. This approach includes teaching social skills; offering play-based learning, moral education, and a greater focus on the arts; and increasing opportunities for students to think for themselves, explore, and create.

HOW CQ SKILLS MAKE THE GRADE

My experience interviewing potential medical students at the university where I teach has reinforced the crucial nature of these CQ skills. Our prospective students come from an incredibly talented pool that includes the highest-ranking undergraduates from universities across North America, trained concert pianists, and Olympic-level athletes. Résumés like these indicate disciplined, hardworking students with high IQs. But for the next generation of physicians, that's no longer enough.

When students are interviewed, their CQ is being assessed. For example, in some interview stations, students are given a painting or a short phrase or poem. They can observe it for one minute; then they have to walk into the room where the examiner is seated and explain what the image or text meant to them and why. They have seven minutes, an eternity for an impromptu speech.

The exercise challenges students to think creatively. It gauges their ability to think on the spot. There's no way to prepare for this type of test, and some students bomb it. One young woman became so stressed she started crying. One young man grew angry; he didn't think it was a fair question. My colleagues call students like these "crispies and teacups"—burned-out or bubble-wrapped students so fragile that they're prone to breaking the moment they encounter an obstacle. These students tend to be risk-averse, exhausted, stressed, and rigid, the precise opposite of what young people should be as they enter medical school.

The applicants who do well, however, are dazzling. They're able to think quickly and communicate beautifully. They look me in the eye. They smile. They speak with passion and authority. They're able to draw from life experience. Their sense of values shines through. *These are the people I'd want as my child's pediatrician*, I think when I come across them.

In teaching medical students (or any other students), we don't need to focus as much on content as we used to. Instead we must put a greater emphasis on teaching them how to think, how to ask the right questions, how to address patients or clients with empathy, how to take initiative, how to solve unanticipated problems creatively, how to cope with real-life stress. And I know the best way to do that.

THE POWER OF PLAY

Play is in our nature. All mammals take time out of their day to play, despite the stress of living in nature where a predator could eat them at any moment. For people of every age, play is directly linked to the development of the brain's prefrontal cortex. That's the front part of the brain that sits directly behind our eyes and directs our highest levels of thinking and functioning.

For the young of all animals, the amount of time spent playing is also directly tied to the rate and size of growth of the cerebellum. The cerebellum, which means "little brain," sits just above the brain stem and is responsible for a number of functions, including motor skills like balance and coordination.

As well, play stimulates nerve growth, promoting new neuron connections between areas that were previously disconnected. Studies have shown that play stimulates neural pathways for abstract thinking, emotional regulation, problem solving, and strategizing. It pushes us to take risks and teaches us how to adapt. In primates, play helps with bonding and reconnection; for example, after a fight, chimpanzees like to tickle each other's palms to show affection and closeness.

But not all play is created equal. Broadly, there are two types: free play and structured play.

Free play is creative and improvised; it helps your child build resilience and contributes to their emotional growth. It also helps them develop problem solving, conflict resolution, and collaboration skills. Playing with stuffies or sand, for example, encourages creativity, imagination, and the healthy expression of feelings. Imaginary play gives kids a chance to act out new situations and see life from other people's perspectives.

Structured play, or goal-oriented play, involves recognizing patterns in order to meet a goal. This includes assembling Lego that includes instructions, a model car, or a spaceship kit, or playing an organized sport like soccer, gymnastics, or hockey.

Both types of play are good for a child's well-being, learning, and growth. But the problem for children whose games are highly structured—for example, those embedded in a software program that makes kids followers instead of leaders—is that they can show deficits in "executive function," meaning the ability to make and carry out plans on their own. The more time children spend in free play, however, the better they develop these capacities.

And so the loss of free play that's been occurring over the last decades—along with the fact that technology has been a big contributor to this loss—is highly concerning.

For example, a 2019 survey of one thousand British nursery workers found that 72 percent believe children today have fewer imaginary friends than they did five years ago, and that 63 percent believe this to be a result of increased screen time. A lot of parents tend to assume that all digital play is play. However, in many cases it's passive structured play, following the software programs of games and apps. In these cases, screens certainly impact creativity by taking time away from opportunities to imagine, invent, innovate, and produce or generate something new or unique. And if children aren't creating neurosynaptic connections for imagination, that part of their brain won't develop.

There are, however, apps and games that encourage free play in kids of all ages. ScratchJr, developed by M.I.T., allows kids to create their own stories, animation, and games. Video games can also loosely fall into free play and structured play categories. For example, *Minecraft* allows kids to build and create a world of their own, in contrast to many first-person shooter games that have them play a single role in an already created world.

The bottom line is that free play provides your children with the cognitive framework and flexible thinking they need to adapt to any situation. As parents, we hear that kids want to "play" on tech all the time. Yet we have to discern what type of play it is and encourage free play. I tell parents to get kids off tech whenever possible—to have them go outside, get rid of rules and structure, and use their beautiful, brilliant minds to play.

Play Builds Creative and Resilient Kids

Creativity and resilience are in fact two sides of the same coin: creative kids tend to be more resilient, and resilient kids tend to be more creative. Creativity means coming up with new ideas and new ways of doing things—and that, after all, is a form of problem-solving resilience.

Creative, resilient kids are smart, happy, and strong. They learn to work at a problem to find the best possible solution, and are often able to imagine entirely new solutions. They know they're strong enough to make it to the other side of an unknown situation because they've done it so many times. They're not afraid of uncertainty or failure. They've learned to adjust to change and misfortune, to persevere when problems arise. They've learned to overcome obstacles. These are all things children develop through unstructured play.

Creativity is both a habit and a state of being. It allows children to see the heart of the problem or to see a situation in a new light—which in turn allows them to make connections between seemingly unrelated things and to gain new perspectives.

PLAY, CREATIVITY, AND CONFIDENCE LOOP VIA SERATONIN

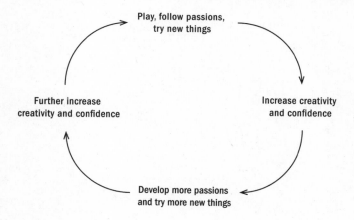

Play, follow passions,
try new things

Increase creativity
and confidence

Develop more passions
and try more new things

Further increase
creativity and confidence

You're probably aware of the "flow state" concept, also known as "being in the zone": the state of mind you get into when you've become completely absorbed in something. Have you ever been working on a project and lost track of time, and of yourself? You were in a flow state! Athletes and artists are always trying to get there. When we're in a flow state our heart rate slows, our anxieties fade, our mood is boosted, and we're free to tap into our creative potential.

A lot of people seem to think that creativity is an innate talent that kids either have or don't have. And while it's true that children are born creators—as I mentioned earlier, it's literally encoded in their DNA—the reality is that creativity is a skill, one that parents and teachers need to help our kids develop. And technology, when used to enhance creativity, lets kids see the world differently, access information from anywhere, and find and develop new passions, concepts, and ideas.

REMEMBER . . .

- Within every child lies a vast reservoir of creative potential.
- No two children have the same thought patterns and brain anatomy. Each is entirely unique, the result of genetic factors and life experiences.
- Owning your future involves understanding and expressing your unique set of skills, talents, and passions.
- Serotonin is an essential neurochemical for creativity—it produces feelings of safety, contentment, and confidence. It also bolsters self-esteem, increases feelings of worthiness, and helps keep anxiety at bay.
- Serotonin is stimulated when we play, when we follow our creative passions and do things we love, when we bond with and contribute to our tribe, and when we exercise and get sunlight.
- Children and teens need guidance to use technology in the six ways to enhance creativity.
- Whereas in the past teaching has focused on content, we now need to put more emphasis on how to think creatively, how to ask the right questions, how to relate to people with empathy, how to take initiative, how to solve unanticipated problems, and how to cope with real-life stress.
- To succeed in a highly social, ultracompetitive, tech-based modern economy, our children need to be equipped with things that computers don't have: cognitive skills like creativity and critical thinking along with the ability to collaborate, communicate, and contribute. These are the five pillars of future-ready intelligence, or CQ.
- When it comes to creativity, free play is more powerful than structured play in that it stimulates neural pathways for abstract thinking, emotional regulation, problem solving, and strategizing.

SOLUTIONS

In this chapter we learned that children are born creators. Technology is allowing them to dream big, see the world differently, access information from anywhere, and find and develop new passions, concepts, and ideas. In developing their identities and individual talents, their minds produce the neurochemical serotonin. This "happy chemical" helps them feel self-respect, pride, and contentment. In the pages ahead I'll suggest ways to help your kids feed their talents and find their life's passions. I'll also suggest how tech can be used to build critical thinking and creativity and to explore, enhance, and showcase their individuality.

KEY STRATEGIES

DON'T

- Solve problems for your kids or bar them from taking risks
- Manage their creativity by hovering over them while they play
- Enrol them in too many structured activities
- Reward them excessively, depriving them of the intrinsic pleasure that comes from making mistakes, failing, and creating
- Eliminate moments of boredom by overscheduling

DO

- Encourage free play and allow for lots of free time
- Be hands off—support self-led problem solving and creativity
- Let your kids make simple choices, whether it's how to do their homework or what to eat for dinner
- Talk about creativity. Ask them questions like *What did you do today that made you think differently?* or *What mistake did you make that taught you something?*
- Guide your child towards different types of play
- Keep learning fun and encourage healthy risk taking
- Encourage them to ask questions and to practise observation

AVOID . . .

Any technology that increases the risk of addiction, stress, anxiety, depression, burnout, perfectionism, and loneliness as it may also reduce the individuality, identity, and passions of your child.

LIMIT AND MONITOR . . .
Play that is strictly structured, resulting in a child passively following another's invention or creativity, as in many video games

ENCOURAGE . . .
Tech that fosters creativity, innovation, connection, and mastery. This kind of tech releases serotonin, and when your child uses tech for creating art, graphics, and websites, or learning to read or do math, they develop greater mastery in these areas.

HOW TO ENHANCE A PLAY MINDSET

Those who have a play mindset are comfortable exploring new ways of doing things, making mistakes, taking risks, and learning through trial and error. All animals learn about the world through trial and error. But even as we parents encourage our children to try new things, we can often send them mixed signals about mistakes and failure. So it's important to remember that the errors are just as important as the trials—and that children who understand and accept failure as just another part of the learning process perform better at school, at work, and in life.

A play mindset, then, is the foundation for adaptability, mastery, creativity, and innovation. Children develop all these through play and exploration. There are at least six subtypes of play, each one developing different centres of the brain. So when we regularly participate in all six types, we develop mastery in different areas of human intelligence and get closer to reaching our full potential. We also develop diversity in both our passions and our talents, allowing us to learn from and be inspired by each other.

1. Storytelling Play

Kids are born storytellers. Indeed, telling stories has been an important part of human culture since our hunter-gatherer days. Storytelling helps us make sense of the world, understand life's lessons, and never forget them.

We can guide children and youth towards tech that helps them practise and master the art of storytelling. They're constantly being exposed to storytelling online—whether in short ads, videos, or articles. But they can create their own books and movies with the help of certain technologies that allow them to accompany their stories with pictures, music, animation, and graphics. You may also want to help your child find opportunities to share their narratives or research. One of our most popular Dolphin Kids camps is a TEDx-style public-speaking camp where kids research a passion and present it to their peers through stories.

2. Body Movement Play

When children move their bodies they're also moving their minds. And when they play—by jumping, falling, running, twirling, throwing, and catching—they're thinking in motion. The push and pull of the physical body that happens in rough-and-tumble play helps develop the pathways for the push and pull of our emotional and social bodies. And it's been found that children who participate in such play—from wrestling to the classic game of Twister—are less likely to bully or be bullied. These games help develop neural trails of understanding how far you can go before someone gets hurt, when to back off, when to assert yourself, and how to say sorry: all critical social skills for later in life.

Guide children towards using technologies that enhance their interest in and mastery of sports, dance, martial arts, yoga, and so forth. Encourage them to choose active technologies like the Nintendo Wii. In moving their bodies in new and different ways, they fire and wire complex neural circuits that enhance their overall IQ, EQ (emotional intelligence), and CQ.

3. Celebratory and Ritual Play

We see this type of play being used hand in hand with technology all the time. Celebrations like International Women's Day and Valentine's Day are played out online via social media and bring enhanced connection and predictability to our lives. Consider all the celebratory and ritual play that happens online every New Year's—messages, memes, videos, quotes, and graphics of inspiration, hope, and resolutions to change old habits and bring in new perspectives. This type of play builds our identity and community connectedness and brings richness to important social patterns.

I myself use celebratory and ritual play in my social media feeds, employing such markers as Motivation Monday, Tech Tuesday, and Wellness Wednesday as a way to maintain a sense of predictability in the information I'm sharing. I also use days of acknowledgment and reverence to celebrate the greater meaning behind a moment, such as being grateful on Remembrance Day or advocating for self-care on World Mental Health Day. Encourage your children to use tech to engage in celebratory and ritual play around the moments and occasions that matter to them.

4. Object Play

The human hand evolved over roughly the same time period as the human brain. We kick off powerful mental processes by using our hands to explore our physical environments. By manipulating objects—whether it's Play-Doh, ceramics, rock sculptures, sandcastles, or video game consoles—your kids are developing pathways that encourage them to explore, to assess their safety, to use different tools. Technology can help them try out other forms of object play. You may want to encourage your child to attempt new things like robotics, drones, and DIY YouTube videos.

5. Educational Play

Educational play involves specific learning, such as reading or math, through trial and error, games, and sheer fun. It tends to be a type of structured play, since it generally has an outcome in the form of an academic lesson or skill.

When your children engage in this kind of play, it's important that they keep in mind the whole point of education: not to beat other people in exams or fill the void of insecurity through awards and accolades, but rather to learn skills that help them gain access to the world around them so that they can create, flourish, make a positive impact, and have fun doing it. That's why they go to school, study, and learn.

Technology that can help them learn skills such as reading and math in the service of building confidence to gain access to the world can generally be considered healthy, as long as it doesn't encroach on a balanced lifestyle.

6. Imaginative Play

Imaginative play is among the most powerful forms of play. When your child allows their mind to wander, they're building new trails of possibility. Imaginative play is linked to creativity, empathy, and higher IQ scores.

I ask my kids to imagine with their senses all the time. What would that idea look like, sound like, feel like? Each time they imagine something they're wiring and firing the link between possibility and reality in their lives.

When my daughter was nervous about starting preschool, I noticed that she naturally used imaginary play to prepare. She pretended she was a teacher, and set up her room like a classroom. I could hear her introducing herself to and "teaching" her imaginary students. She continues to repeat this practice for all sorts of new possibilities—taking her first dive in swim practice, changing elementary schools, singing in a choir. In doing so she builds new trails and wires and fires possibility into reality.

VISUALIZATION

As children get older, they often stop playing imaginary games—but they don't have to. And one way to encourage tweens and teens to continue imaginative play is through visualization.

Visualization is a powerful way to de-stress—to reduce cortisol, release endorphins, and initiate new trails of confidence and creativity through serotonin. It can also help your child meet their concrete, practical goals.

A lot of anxiety we may feel about something is grounded in the uncertainty or unfamiliarity of the experience. And since we know that the human brain doesn't always differentiate between a real memory and an imagined one, we can help our children use visualization to familiarize their mind with the activity and build confidence in trying new and different things. For example, one of my sons is afraid of heights, so I guided him towards using visualization to reduce his fears and prepare for a ziplining adventure we had planned.

If you can create a clear, confident image of yourself in a situation by building a full, positive visualization of the sights, sounds, smells, and feelings you might experience in being successful at it, you'll often be able to translate that positive "memory" to real life confidence and success. This kind of visualization can also help kids develop new skills more quickly: my kids use it to improve their three-point shots in basketball!

HOW TO GUIDE YOUR CHILD
THROUGH A VISUALIZATION EXERCISE

1. Ask your child to relax their body and mind through a few minutes of deep, relaxed breathing.
2. Help them determine their visualization goal clearly: *I'm going to imagine successfully delivering my speech in public.*
3. Help your child make the scene as real as possible. Ask them to try using all their senses to build up a realistic scene—a "memory" that will remain vivid in their mind: *"See yourself in front of the audience and feel the lights on your face and the microphone in your hands."*
4. Have them evoke positive emotions by visualizing past or future moments of joy, gratitude, love, and pride, allowing the release of dopamine, endorphins, oxytocin, and serotonin to solidify pathways. You might expand the scene your child is visualizing by saying something like *"Now imagine how your body is going to feel when*

you're giving your speech—how excited and happy you're going to be. You've spent weeks writing and practising your speech and so you're comfortable here, sharing your knowledge with the audience. Look out at the audience and see how engaged they are, how this information can help them. Take a moment to enjoy it and to take pride in your accomplishment. You worked hard, and now here you are; you did it." The more vivid the details, the better for reducing stress and wiring positive feelings with the activity.

5. Repeat for best results!

KEEP LEARNING FUN

In criticizing children when they make a mess, for example constantly evaluating them through report cards, and s ized tests, we condition them to avoid play. Conversely positive emotions like wonder, pride, and joy to a task task with endorphins, serotonin, and many other power chemicals, including oxytocin if it's a social activity. And twenty-first century requires lifelong learning, we must fi wire learning with fun and positive emotion if we want ou dren to be self-motivated.

Cultivating a sense of fun around learning can help your child remain engaged and intrinsically motivated in their day-to-day life. This will certainly translate to all aspects of their life—and will help them remain curious and engaged in continuing to learn about the tech that will shape their futures.

Thankfully, many practices that keep learning fun are the very things children love to do. They're a part of play, which means we don't need any special training to do them. I call these "CQ developers" because they encourage the five pillars of the Consciousness Quotient: creativity, critical thinking, communication, collaboration, and contribution. Here are some of my favourites.

Encourage Questions and Observation

Asking questions and observing the world are things children do naturally and quite expertly: *Why is the sky blue? Why does the sun rise on this side and set on that side? Why do you have to go to work? Why do people have to die? Why, why, why . . . ?* Children who question anything and everything have a passion for critical thinking, challenging the status quo, and pushing boundaries.

So make a conscious effort to celebrate your child's curiosity from a young age. While it may be tempting to shut down excessive questioning, asking questions builds crucial critical thinking skills that will serve them when they're older. Try to see the world through their eyes, and offer up an enthusiastic and engaged response—even if you've been asked "Why?" a hundred times that day.

As your children get older and start to explore the online world, guide them towards observing and questioning what they're seeing online. *What is the point of that video, meme, or image? How could technology be used to express an idea or concept?* Not only will this foster critical thinking and creativity, it will also arm your kids with a stronger ability to make good judgments and quick decisions that will keep them safe. And by having experienced your consistent interest in their curiosity when they were young, they'll have built that neural trail and will know they can go to you with any questions that come up online. But like all habits, they have to continue to use the associated trail, so remember to ask them questions and remind them to turn to you as well.

Have Children Try First Before You Step In

Sometimes it's good to let children try something before offering them any instruction or advice. Be encouraging, and tell them that there's no right or wrong way, so try it their way! This open-ended exploration of the world creates neural trails of comfort with uncertainty, abstract thinking, problem solving, and hands-on learning.

For example, if your child's tech consumption gets out of balance, encourage them to brainstorm and try out ideas to redress that imbalance. Once they have, you can collaboratively evaluate their approach and what may help them further succeed. Then have them try again—and repeat this process until they can solve the problem on their own. Since kids have a deep knowledge of tech use, tips, and tools, you may be surprised by what they come up with. For example, when I reminded my nine-year-old daughter that her goal was to cut down on mindless YouTube videos in favour of more creative platforms, she came up with four delightful programs that helped her create her own movie, music video, wall mosaic, and lip gloss!

This concept is also key to establishing healthy learning habits. My son used to want help finding the right sites to visit for research before he'd even tried on his own. I explained that homework isn't only about following instructions or getting the answer right or wrong—it's also about figuring out what you already know and what you need to learn.

So instead of supplying the answer, try breaking things down for them. Suppose, for example, that your child is frustrated over a particular homework problem she's been trying to solve. Instead of showing her how to do it, ask her where she's stuck and why. Then encourage her to break down the problem into small steps. Try giving her a clue or a small suggestion. As she progresses through resolving the problem, say things like "You're really close" or, if she gets stuck, "I can help you with this part." This approach will help initiate their critical thinking, adaptability, and innovation pathways and move children from being followers to being leaders.

Encourage Healthy Risk Taking

Guide your children to be curious, to try new things, to take risks. Take precautions with new technologies, however. Tell your kids to be careful when trying out new things online. It may be okay to try a new way of writing through a blog or by designing a website, but it wouldn't be wise to post something that could be embarrassing later on, like a deeply personal story or a photo depicting a party.

For teens who are already risk takers, I wouldn't recommend using tech as a platform for risk taking, since they may be stuck with a permanent record of something they'll later regret. Instead, encourage them to try a new sport, hobby, or art form, like a drama or an improv class. They could also take risks by going to an amusement park or watching a horror movie.

THE DOs AND DON'Ts OF TAKING RISKS ONLINE

DO

- Follow the golden rule: treat others in the same way you would want to be treated in the online world.
- Think about the future before you write or post anything. There's no such thing as a true delete from the internet, and content can be easily spread and altered.

- Work with your child to determine privacy settings on their social media accounts. Show them how to restrict who sees their posts, photos, and messages, and explain why.
- Remind your child that you're here to talk if there's ever cause for concern, and that you'll always respond out of love, not a desire to punish them.

DON'T

- Share personal information, including passwords, online
- Respond to emails, texts, or messages from strangers
- Turn on location sharing
- Click links, open attachments, or accept gifts from someone you don't know
- Agree to meet someone you met online
- Use fake birthdates to gain access to apps. The U.S. Children's Online Privacy and Protection Act forbids online companies from knowingly collecting data and using it for marketing purposes on users under thirteen.

REMEMBER DOWNTIME!

According to the well-known tale, the mathematician Archimedes was sinking into a public bath in ancient Greece, stewing over a problem, when it suddenly struck him that the more his body was submerged into the water, the more water slipped over the side. When the math whiz realized he'd hit on the answer he'd been searching for, he leapt up and rushed home naked, yelling "Eureka! Eureka!" What he'd discovered was a way to measure volume by displacement.

History is full of moments like these. Isaac Newton, lounging in the shade, was bonked by a falling apple and discovered gravity. And Albert Einstein, while chatting idly with a good friend, developed a key insight into his theory of relativity.

Research conducted by Jonathan Schooler, who teaches brain science at the University of California at Santa Barbara, underlines that these inspirational lightning strikes happen only when we allow our brains to roam—in other words, that our brains need free time to drift in order to make unexpected neuronal connections.

Just imagine, I tell my kids, if on that fateful day Archimedes had spent his bathtime scrolling his Instagram feed.

8

INTUITION: Guiding Your Family to a Healthy Tech Diet

Tell me what you eat, and I will tell you what you are.

—ANTHELME BRILLAT-SAVARIN

MY MOM, GIAN, IS EIGHTY-TWO. She worked for decades as a cook, cleaner, and factory worker while raising five kids. One of eight siblings herself, she grew up in a small village in the Punjab. Although she was bright and quick, sending her to school was beyond her parents' means. Gian endured a lot of hardship throughout her life, but she always maintained a sense of grace, hope, and gratitude. She trusts that the universe has her back and that all will work out the way it was meant to. In her Sikh faith, three beliefs are paramount: you work hard, you share with your community, and you trust in your spiritual connection, especially in difficult times.

On Sundays at the temple after prayers, we'd help our mother make lunch for the community and then clean up afterwards. Even when I was stressed about having an assignment due or an exam the following day, my mom wouldn't let me beg off: she'd always say that my community needed me. This gave me not only a sense that my actions mattered, but also an understanding of the greater good. Contribution and trust were key values in our home. I remember once getting 95 percent on a difficult math exam and rushing home to tell my mom. "That's good," she said. "But what did you do in your day? Who did you help?" She would always make sure I understood that there was more to life than academic or material success.

We were by no means wealthy, and yet, even when we were just getting by, my parents showed us we could trust that our future had enough to share. Once, when my father was driving a taxi, he met a newly arrived immigrant at the airport. The man had nowhere to stay, so my dad invited him to our home, where he remained for two years. My parents taught us that the strongest bonds survive because when there is suffering, we share. That a life of purpose is built on kindness, compassion, trust, and community.

My mom didn't fret about the right way to parent when we were growing up (in fact, she thinks the whole idea of a parenting expert is baloney). Gian is a grounded woman who used common sense to guide her actions. She had high expectations for us, but trusted us to do the work and succeed on our own volition. She had rules and structure, but she didn't micromanage us. She expected us to do our best in school, but rarely checked to see whether we'd finished our homework. In short, she was a true dolphin parent.

Dolphin parents provide children with an environment that sends the message of trust: that it's okay to fall and be clumsy. And this is how we learn best—through trial and error. When children are young, dolphin parents pick them up and help them clean up after themselves. They encourage independence. As their children grow older, they guide them to learn to pick themselves up and clean up their own messes. They value self-care, connection, adaptability, community, and self-motivation.

My mom was parenting by intuition, the knowledge gifted to us by nature. She knew intuitively that trust, optimism, contribution, and a balanced lifestyle were key to a healthy life. To flourish in today's hyperconnected, stressful world, I think we need to remember these simple truths more than ever. Of course, I'm not saying that parenting is a passive process. It's not okay to grant your child unlimited access to technology by buying them an iPhone or a laptop and hoping they figure it out. The hard work of parenting involves consistently guiding your children in becoming the best version of themselves.

In this chapter I offer you a straightforward parenting paradigm to help guide your children towards better digital decision making. By now you understand what's happening in their mind when they're using tech and how tech will impact them, now and in the future. You understand the ways tech companies are exploiting human biology to keep kids hooked on their products. But you also know that healthy technology can help children connect, create, and flourish.

Before we get to my six-week, six-step plan for rebalancing your family's tech use, let me return to the idea of using intuition to help guide your decision making.

THE BEAUTY OF INTUITION

Think back to the last time you binged on junk food all alone in your kitchen or in front of the TV. You might have felt a rush of excitement when you reached for those cookies. That sensation was caused by dopamine. And how did you feel when the cookies were all gone? Were you craving more? Perhaps, but I bet you were also feeling a bit grumpy, frustrated with yourself, and maybe even a bit sick. That feeling was caused by a combination of dopamine withdrawal and cortisol. Now, think back to the last time you cooked or ate a healthy meal with your family. Did you feel any guilt or frustration when you finished? Likely not. In fact, I bet the meal left you feeling content, bonded to the people closest to you, and perhaps even motivated to tackle the next task at hand. Those good feelings were caused by the release of endorphins, oxytocin, and serotonin.

Our bodies are always communicating with us, whether we choose to listen or not. When you drink a third glass of wine, get clumsy, and start slurring your words, your body is telling you to stop drinking. When you start to feel sick after eating a second piece of chocolate cake, your body is telling you to dial it back.

The reality is, you didn't need a book or an expert to explain all that. If you were relaxed and reflective, you understood what your body was communicating to you. That's intuition. If you were feeling stressed out, triggering your freeze-fight-or-flight response, however, all you'd be feeling is anxiety, irritability, and distraction. You wouldn't be able to hear what your body was communicating to you. It would all be conflicting noise. You'd be bouncing around. Rather than intuitively interacting with your world, you'd be reacting to it—driven by your survival instincts.

To me, intuition is synonymous with common sense—knowledge we all share, grounded in the neurochemical system and neuroplastic hardwiring I've discussed in preceding chapters. It's when we're relaxed that we can best access how we intuitively feel about a situation. Answers and solutions will be clear.

The experience of consuming tech isn't all that different from eating, and triggers similar biological responses. Certain types of tech nurture your children's minds and bodies while others leave them feeling awful, especially if they overindulge. By paying attention to their experiences with technology and encouraging them to make a habit of doing the same, they can begin to cultivate their own intuition about the tech they're consuming and, in time, learn how to self-regulate.

WHAT IS A HEALTHY TECH DIET?

Education is another important part of learning to self-regulate. A healthy tech diet involves educating your children in self-regulation by teaching them to view the technology they consume the same way they do the food they eat. After all, it impacts their bodies and minds in similar ways. Just as we teach our kids to avoid toxic foods, limit snack foods, and focus on healthy foods, we must also teach them to avoid toxic tech, limit junk tech, and consume healthy technology as part of a balanced life. And just ass brain-boosting foods like wild salmon, nuts, and berries will help them function at a higher level, brain-boosting tech will allow them to do the same.

This type of teaching—based on a familiar paradigm, beginning early, and building over time—is likely to stay with your children for their entire lives. And in teaching your child about tech alongside nutrition, you'll also elevate technology consumption to the importance you give to healthy eating.

We know, however, that just as food can't always be easily divided into simple categories—granola bars, for example, might seem healthy but are often heavily processed and high in sugar—the same holds true for technology. That's why the Tech Solution that follows doesn't categorize technology as either good or bad but considers the context it's used in, what neurochemicals it releases, and how it makes children feel. Tech consumed in the middle of the night, for example, when it gets in the way of sleep, is never healthy, and nor is tech used as an escape from feeling stressed or agitated. Having conversations about these things with your kids will help them understand how their tech use impacts their emotions and behaviours, and will, in turn, help them make their own healthy choices.

In fact, this type of "neuro education" will open the door to deeper insights into a range of human experiences. Your children will begin to understand that their feelings, moods, and behaviours are affected not only by the foods they eat and the tech they consume but also by the relationships they build and how they choose to spend their time.

1. Healthy Tech

Healthy tech encompasses the kinds of websites, apps, and platforms that will lead your children's brains to release endorphins, oxytocin, or serotonin. Put differently, this is tech that will lead them to what you might think of as the three C's: (self-)care, connection, and creation. With healthy tech you can be flexible and let your kids enjoy exploring the world online, as long as their time is balanced with other healthy real-life habits (see How to Schedule Tech Time, pages 46–7). I encourage my kids to use their tech time to either care for themselves, connect with others, or be creative. Tell your kids it's like eating healthy fruits, vegetables, and proteins.

So let's review these key ingredients to self-care, connection, and creation:

Endorphins are the body's natural painkiller and a neurochemical of well-being and euphoria. Tech use that promotes forms of **self-care** such as mindfulness, gratitude, and cardiovascular exercise will stimulate the endorphin system.

Oxytocin makes us feel warm and fuzzy inside when we make meaningful **connections** and build bonds with others. Examples of tech that will trigger the release of oxytocin include FaceTiming with family and friends, positive social media, and community-building activities like online advocacy or fundraising. Oxytocin release from these types of tech is generally healthy. One exception is when marketers and bad actors manipulate trust to promote agendas and encourage spending. So it's important to not assume that all feelings of online bonding and trust are healthy, and to teach children to be aware and critical of manipulation tactics.

Serotonin—the neurochemical of creativity, happiness, and confidence—is released when we use tech that allows us to **create**, innovate, and develop mastery in an area of interest. For example, when your child uses tech to create art, graphics, and websites, or when learning to read or do math, they're developing greater mastery of these skills and art forms. Participation in online activities that result in creative thinking, independent problem solving, and leadership is also healthy.

2. Junk Tech

Dopamine—the neurochemical of reward—encourages humans to hunt, gather, and bond in the short term. Its release can be positive if those activities are kept in balance and lead to the activation of the oxytocin, serotonin, and endorphin systems. We do this through (self-)care, connection, and creativity: the three C's I cited earlier. But dopamine is a lot like sugar. We need it to survive, but too much of it can cause addictions and other harm.

Examples of junk tech include superficially socializing (or bonding) by maintaining a Snapchat streak or scrolling and liking social media. Dopamine can be released while playing video games like *Halo* (hunting) or *Candy Crush Saga* (gathering), especially when your kids are playing alone. Consuming this type of tech use is no different from eating chips or candy. Dopamine will certainly be released from the competition, collection, or perceived socializing, but without more meaningful activities, the sense of withdrawal children experience after putting down the console or iPad will cause them to want to return to the activity for another hit of dopamine. This can set up the feedback loop where junk tech becomes toxic, addictive, or stressful tech. However, working with your child to attune them to how this tech is making them feel in the short and long term will be highly beneficial in helping them self-regulate, make positive choices, and establish healthy habits.

I look at junk tech the same way I do treats. If kept to a minimum, it won't harm your child. On Fridays, for example, I might let my kids eat pizza for dinner and have chips or ice cream later on. My daughter is allowed to watch one hour of her favourite YouTube show and my sons get to play *NBA Live* or *FIFA* with their cousins. But if that's all they were consuming throughout the week, it would have serious health repercussions.

So just as too much sugar can become toxic, junk tech can become toxic tech in two ways:

1. When its use has gotten out of control and addictive habits develop. Any tech use in this context is toxic. It needs to be managed and/or treated.

2. When its use takes time away from the three C's—(self-)care, connection, and creativity. Even when your child isn't addicted to video games or social media, if the time they're spending on this type of media interferes with the three C's, that tech use has become toxic.

Since avoiding junk tech entirely probably isn't realistic, discuss, limit, and monitor video games and social media until your child seems able to regulate their own use of it. As with junk food, the less you bring into the home and expose your child to, the better.

3. Toxic Tech

Toxic tech is any tech use that causes the release of cortisol—the neurochemical of stress and a hallmark of our sleep-deprived, overly busy, distracted, and increasingly lonely society. Cortisol pushes your children to withdraw socially, dysregulates such biological rhythms as sleep and appetite, and clouds their thinking. Any technology that leads to the release of cortisol is toxic. Your children should try their best to avoid it completely.

Examples of toxic tech include cyberbullying, online social conflicts, and social media that leads to FOMO and comparisons. Keep in mind that multitasking—constantly shuffling through media by opening and closing Twitter, Snapchat, Instagram, *BuzzFeed*, a podcasting app, a chat, and so on—can also be toxic. We must teach our kids that when tech isn't being implemented intentionally for productivity and efficiency, we develop the bad habit of engaging in continual partial attention. Not only is this stressful, but it also doesn't foster the reflection, contemplation, and focus that help us learn and accomplish our goals.

Stay firm when guiding your children towards eliminating and avoiding toxic tech. I try not to buy or allow my kids to use it at all: we block all potential gambling and pornography sites, and with our older kids I frequently check in and discuss the toxicity of FOMO, online comparisons, and unintentional multitasking.

Remember, the consumption of even healthy tech can trigger the stress response if it leads to a prolonged lack of eye contact with others, sleep deprivation, sedentary behaviour, posture issues, or loneliness. Tech use should always either facilitate or, at the very least, not interfere with the essential ingredients of a healthy, balanced life—the activities that lead to the release of oxytocin (when kids build meaningful bonds), endorphins (when they practise self-care), and serotonin (when they engage in creative pursuits).

BUILDING A HEALTHY TECH DIET

On the following pages I've included a handy reference chart to help you categorize different types of tech usage. (But remember: always use your intuition to determine whether something healthy or fun in moderation has turned into junk or toxic tech that may have harmful effects.)

Key Neurochemicals	Avoid Toxic Tech	Limit and Monitor Junk Tech	Enjoy Healthy Tech in Moderation
Dopamine	· gambling · pornography addictive use of: · video games · social media · shopping	· video games with persuasive design · mindless tech with no purpose; e.g., scrolling · superficial social media; e.g., Snapchat streaks, gathering likes	
Cortisol	tech use that leads to: · social comparison · FOMO · social conflict · cyberbullying · multitasking · sleep deprivation · lack of eye contact · loneliness · sedentary behaviour · poor posture		
Endorphins			tech use that leads to self-care as long as it's balanced with real-life activities, including: · exercise · mindfulness/meditation · gratitude · sleep
Oxytocin	tech that manipulates and exploits a child's trust and bonding, such as: · toxic friends · predators · scammers · political extremism		tech use that leads to social connection, as long as it's balanced with real-life activities: · video chat with loved ones · positive social media chat · community building · advocacy fundraising

Key Neurochemicals	Avoid Toxic Tech	Limit and Monitor Junk Tech	Enjoy Healthy Tech in Moderation
Serotonin			tech use that leads to creativity and confidence, as long as it's balanced with real-life activities: · educational sites, such as "learn-to-read" or math sites · art-based activities, including drawing, building websites, iMovie, graphic design · coding and creating video games, apps, etc. · informative webinars, online courses (e.g., MasterClass)

Put it all together, and a healthy tech diet might look something like this:

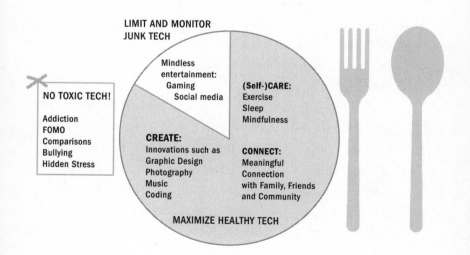

PARENTING FOR A HEALTHY TECH DIET

The best way to guide your children towards healthy tech use is to behave as a dolphin parent and be firm yet flexible (page 33). Even with healthy tech—and always with junk tech!—we need to watch our children's portion sizes and help guard them from overindulging, especially those who are prone to it. Help your kids learn to "listen to their tummies" by encouraging them to reflect on how their tech consumption is making them feel. That way they'll know when to turn off the screen. Remember, it's parents who control the supply lines—we're the ones who make the purchases that determine what kids indulge in, and when.

Of course, there will always be slip-ups. And you'll find that you need to make tweaks and adjustments, just as you do with your kids' diets. If my kids want to play a video game longer or watch TV during the week, they have to ask us, just as they have to ask for extra dessert. And believe me, there are times when they don't ask! When they're caught, we talk about it. Sometimes we take away the video game or remove the privilege of watching TV. Sometimes the Xbox console or iPad gets stored in our bedroom. We sometimes do the same with all of the junk food in the house.

Just as we advise parents to delay junk food for infants and alcohol for teens as long as possible, do the same for junk tech. If your sixteen-year-old isn't drinking, don't give her a beer. Don't normalize it. If your six-year-old isn't begging to go online, don't introduce him to an iPad. There's no rush. Keep in mind that there's no evidence to support introducing technology at an early age. And just as you limit sweets in the real world, talk with your kids about setting limits with tech.

Understand, though, that holidays and other special circumstances will require some flexibility. If you're flying with a five-
year-old, the world won't end if you entertain them with an
iPad or let them have an extra cookie—or both!

THE TECH SOLUTION: A SIX-WEEK, SIX-STEP PLAN

I've developed this structured plan for establishing a healthy tech diet for you and your family. Yes, I said you and your family! We know that change works best through a group process. It doesn't single out a "problem" individual, and members can provide one another with support, motivation, and momentum.

The plan includes evidence-based steps that I've researched, taught, and used in my clinical practice for almost twenty years. They're grounded in the science of motivational interviewing, cognitive behavioural therapy, and common sense. I've tried, tested, and finessed these steps with countless children, teens, and adults—some of whom had serious addictions. The steps may look simple, but remember, simple isn't always easy. It will require your ongoing attention, as all successful parenting does, but I promise that when you apply this process consistently to the technology you consume, you'll see change. For some, changes will occur quickly. For others, it will take time. Do your best to be understanding, and to walk shoulder to shoulder with your child every step of the way. And if you would like to receive a weekly email that will prompt you with the worksheets and graphics from this section (and more!), visit www.dolphinkids.ca/techsolution.

THE STAGES OF CHANGE

There's a lot of truth to the adage that change is a process. Back in the early 1980s psychology professors James Prochaska and Carlo DiClemente developed the Stages of Change model—and it has since become key to understanding where people come from in relation to making healthy lifestyle changes. Here we'll use it as a framework to describe the five phases your family will progress through as you transform your tech diet.

Understanding the hurdles you and your family face, and gaining insight into each person's mindset, wherever they are in the process of changing their behaviour, will help you support them through this plan and keep them on the path to achieving their goals. Some families may be able to move through the six steps in less than six weeks. For others, certain steps may take more than a week, and that's okay—what's important is to be sequential—do one step at a time—and keep guiding your children to move on to the next step. Remember to be patient and to remain attuned to how your kids are feeling. And don't wait until the finish line to celebrate the small changes you're noticing, whether it's your son going a week without gaming or your teen's healthier attitude to social media.

As you prepare your family for this six-week challenge, consider what stage you, your co-parent, and your kids are in before you begin. This will help you provide the appropriate support as you guide everyone to a healthier relationship with tech.

STAGES OF CHANGE MODEL

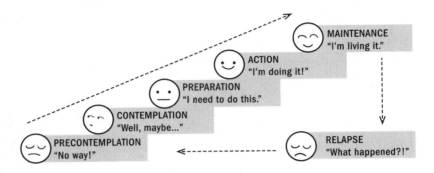

If you think back to a time when you made a change—perhaps you quit smoking or built a habit of cycling to work—some of these stages may sound pretty familiar.

Consider, for example, how long you thought about making a change before you actually took steps to do it. And if you've ever sat down to talk about homework or chores with your family, you were probably already in the action stage. The same will likely be true when you sit down to talk about screen time and changing your family's tech diet. You've read this book, thought about the pros and cons of making a change, and will already be armed with a plan (the one you're reading right now). The rest of your family, however, will likely be in one of two stages: precontemplation or contemplation.

As a parent, your role is to understand where they are and to help guide them towards change. This is exactly what the Tech Solution is designed to do.

Before we begin, let's consider an example of a teenage daughter deciding to cut back on social media. Here's how it might go.

In the **precontemplation** stage, she may be thinking, *Healthy tech? Nope. Not for me. I love Instagram. And I can't live without Snapchat.*

Then along comes **contemplation**: *I really want to get on Instagram and see what's happening online, but I should do my homework, or I might fail that class . . .*

After a while, **determination/preparation** sets in, usually based on new information: *I failed the last assignment. If I don't start doing my homework I'm going to fail that class. I really need to dial back the time I'm wasting online.*

Next come **action** and **maintenance**, maybe in the form of a whole month spent off social media and handing in her assignments on time.

But then she might hit a speed bump—whether it's a bad grade or the sense that she's missing out on memes, jokes, and conversations. Uh-oh, along comes . . . **relapse**: *I'm never going to pass anyway. I need a break. I need to blow off some steam.* And back she goes to social media.

The ideal outcome is to get to the point where you and your family are able to sit comfortably in the maintenance stage. Still, relapse is part of the Stages of Change model, so you may find that you or your children relapse more than once over the course of changing your family's tech diet. That's completely normal.

When it does happen, though, it's important to know that you or your child may re-enter the process in different places. You may find that your relapse period is short and you're quickly ready for action again, but that your child may need some time off to reconsider their goals. Pay close attention, and listen to your child—that way you can support them until they're able to uphold their ideal behaviour with relative consistency and remain in the maintenance stage in the long term. This will allow a full rewiring of old habits and neural pathways, ultimately leading to transformation and long-term change.

WEEK 1: BUILD MOTIVATION

When it comes to tech use, many kids will be in the **precontemplation** stage. They won't see any reason to change their tech consumption, and may deny that there's even a problem. The goal of this step is to get your family to start thinking hard about the impact tech is having on their lives.

Get them thinking about their tech use by:

- Having open-ended conversations about their screen time that help you understand what they like and don't like about the tech in their lives
- Validating their feelings about not wanting to reduce their gaming or the time they're spending on social media
- Introducing the idea of a healthy tech diet; explaining how their experiences with technology release neurochemicals in their brains; explaining how this impacts their behaviours and feelings
- Encouraging them to evaluate their current tech diet; discussing the pros and cons of cutting back; trying to be empathetic, not judgmental
- Asking whether they would consider that kind of change

- Being a role model and reducing your own tech use
- Making your intention for a family tech reset clear

Once you've had these conversations, it's time to evaluate the reasons your family would like to change their tech diet. Remember that your children are individuals, and that the more you reach out and listen to them about their tech consumption, the better equipped you'll be to support their unique needs. Each of you needs to be clear about how much tech you're currently consuming and how much you want to reduce it. The more open and honest you are about your own tech use, the more your children are likely to open up and be truthful about their own. That clarity will be an anchor to which you can return whenever motivation wavers.

Use the following motivational assessment worksheet to help you and your children explore the reasons for improving your tech diet. It's normal to have mixed feelings when we're making changes. Discussing tech's pros and cons is a great way to get your children thinking and talking about the way they engage with tech.

For example, ask your son what he likes about video gaming. He might tell you that it helps him with problem solving and builds his coordination. Then ask him about the *downsides* of gaming. I bet you'll be surprised by how much he has to say. This is the first step towards really understanding what's going on in your child's mind—and it's only through such understanding that we can be effective in guiding them to change.

I suggest introducing this worksheet when you and your family first come together to talk about your tech use. Let them know that you'll fill it out together at the end of Week 1. To give you some ideas for filling in the blanks on your own worksheet, I've completed the one below the way my own family would.

MOTIVATION ASSESSMENT WORKSHEET

Consider your family's current tech use. What is and isn't working well? Instead of simply listing what kind of tech your family uses, be sure to zero in on the specific *benefits* and *drawbacks* for each category listed below.

Physical Health
Benefits:
- Music encourages us to exercise and have fun, especially when we have kitchen dance parties.
- Mom watches yoga YouTube videos, Jaever follows circuit training on YouTube, Gia uses her fitness tracker every day, and Dad counts his steps and heart rate when working out—so tech helps guide and encourage us to be active.
- Coaches send videos of plays for Joesh and Jaever to watch in preparation for games to ensure that they know the team strategies.

Drawbacks:
- We all sit way too much! Video games, TV, phone, and computer use lead to hunched posture, neck/back pain, and being sedentary. It often leads to eating junk food too.
- Mom and Joesh are night owls, and can lose track of time when they're on screens at night for homework, work, or entertainment. This affects their sleep, which makes them cranky in the morning and tired through the day.

Mental Health
Benefits:

- We all use guided meditations from iTunes or the Spark app. Joesh and Jaever sometimes meditate with the Muse device, too.
- Parents pick movies that build character, and we have family discussions about integrity, community, and resiliency around them.
- Sometimes we watch comedy movies or skits from late-night TV, like *A Little Late with Lily Singh*, for a good family laugh.

Drawbacks:

- Hearing about bad things happening in the world on news sites and social media can be stressful.
- Some of us definitely feel FOMO, especially when we see friends having fun online. On rainy days we sometimes feel worse about our weather when we see people living in sunny places. We try not to compare our lives to all the wonderful things we see people doing online. We know it's filtered reality, but it can still lead to feeling as though our lives aren't amazing enough.

Social Health
Benefits:

- Cousin and friend chat groups are so much fun! They help everyone stay connected, even though there are so many different groups.
- Mom enjoys staying connected with her business partners in India and seeing what the kids are doing there, and we all stay connected with international friends and family via WhatsApp.
- It can be hilarious trying to teach grandparents how to use a smartphone or a computer!

Drawbacks:

- A lot of conflicts around phone use and video gaming can occur, especially on holidays and during the summer when we're out of our usual routine. This really affects the whole family.
- Sometimes we're all in our own rooms on our computers, so we can miss important parts of other people's day and not spend enough time with each other.
- It takes a lot of time and can be stressful communicating with friends and family online—it can sometimes feel like a full-time job that's never done.

WEEK 2: PREPARE FOR ACTION

This week you're preparing your family to change their tech diet. By this point your child is willing to consider that their tech habits *may* benefit from change, but they may still be conflicted and are likely not yet ready to act. They might say something like "I know I spend too much time gaming and that my sports are suffering, but I just don't want to cut down."

Try supporting them by:

- Encouraging them to think further about the advantages and disadvantages of having a healthier tech diet
- Telling them about the benefits of a new tech diet
- Brainstorming ways they might change
- Helping them think through potential obstacles

Ask things like:

- What could happen to your sports if you don't cut back on gaming?
- Were you able to self-regulate your social media use at Grandma's house last summer vacation?
- How can you still play video games and not let it impact your sports or schoolwork?

The Motivation Ruler

As you and your family move closer to making changes to your tech diet, you may find that your children are lacking motivation. Not to worry! Assessing their motivation, and understanding why they might be running low on it, will help you get them on track.

Generally, research shows that motivation tends to wane for the following two reasons:

1. Your child believes that the change isn't important.

2. Your child has a lack of confidence that change is possible.

The motivation ruler is a great tool to help your children evaluate how important changing their tech diet is to them, and how confident they feel in their ability to change.

Have your kids figure out their scores on the rulers below. Are they lacking confidence in their ability to change? Or are they struggling to decide whether change is even important to them?

HOW IMPORTANT IS IT TO YOU TO HAVE A HEALTHIER TECH DIET?

0   1   2   3   4   5   6   7   8   9   10

Not important   Somewhat   Extremely
    at all   important   important

HOW CONFIDENT ARE YOU THAT YOU CAN CHANGE YOUR TECH DIET?

0   1   2   3   4   5   6   7   8   9   10

Not confident   Somewhat   Extremely
    at all   confident   confident

If their score for the importance of change is beneath 3, more work needs to be done exploring the reasons to change. Try reminding them about the impact of technology on their bodies and minds, drawing specific examples from their own lives. Ask them what might happen if they don't change.

If their score for their confidence in their ability to change is beneath 3, more work needs to be done on how to make the change. Ask them to think about the efforts they're going to make—can they visualize their success (see Visualization, pages 220–22)? Acknowledge any progress you've noticed. Offer extra support. Tell them stories about other kids who changed or a behaviour you once managed to change. Ask them if there's anything getting in the way of change, and build their confidence by giving them specific solutions to problems or obstacles they might face.

Ask your kids: Why did you choose a 7 and not a 5 when it comes to your confidence in your ability to change? What would it take for you to move to an 8 or a 9? These questions will help them walk upon the neural trails of confidence and help them feel that they really can change.

It's possible that it will take more than one week for your child's motivation to reach a point where it pushes them to take action along with the rest of the family. Once motivation reaches at least a 5 for both importance and confidence, your child is likely ready to move on to the next step.

WEEK 3: TAKE ACTION

This week is about moving from preparation to action by setting goals.

Support your family by:

- Reminding them that you're all in it together, and that in order to be successful everyone will have to pull their weight
- Helping them establish SMART goals (see page 254-55)
- Making the moment of action fun by setting up a challenge that encourages healthy competition among members of your family or community
  - Sign up for a #techdietchallenge at www.dolphinkids.ca /techsolution and participate with friends, families, and schools. Here you'll find additional materials like a pledge card and certificates of completion that you can print off and use to keep motivation high.

At the beginning of the week, each member of the family should come up with three to five SMART goals regarding their tech use. Encourage your kids to keep it simple.

SMART goals are goals that are:

Specific: Ask your kids what exactly they want to achieve and why they want to achieve it. Specific goals could include reducing the time they spend gaming or increasing the time they spend on math games and fitness apps.

Measurable: Have your kids come up with measurable goals, like spending a maximum of fifteen minutes on healthy social media during weekdays. To help them self-regulate, teach them to use screen time trackers on their phones and tablets and show them how to set reminders to help keep them on target.

Achievable: Make sure your kids are coming up with realistic goals. I often suggest that my kids need to actually reduce their grand goals—like no TV for a month, a hundred push-ups every day, or the really crazy one of showering without reminders!

Relevant: Ask your kids whether their goal seems worthwhile. Will it help them have more free time, become happier, or help improve their emotional health?

Time-bound: Encourage your kids to set a start date and a completion date for each of their goals.

Use the template below to help your family come up with their SMART goals for healthier tech use.

	SPECIFIC:	
S	What healthy tech do I want to consume more of?	
	What junk tech do I want to limit and monitor?	
	What toxic tech do I want to avoid?	
M	MEASURABLE:	
	How will I measure my progress?	
	How will I know when the goal is accomplished?	
A	ACHIEVABLE:	
	What are the logical steps I need to take?	
	Do I have the necessary resources?	
	What will help/hinder my achievement?	
R	RELEVANT:	
	Why is this a worthwhile goal?	
	Is this the right time to make this change?	
	Is this goal in line with my long-term plans?	
T	TIME-BOUND:	
	How long will it take to accomplish this goal?	
	When am I aiming to start/complete this goal?	
	When am I going to work on this goal?	

Now that you've done all the prep work—learned about the stages of change; evaluated the pros and cons of your tech diet; understood the importance of, and have confidence in, change; and compiled your SMART goals—it's time for everyone to commit to a healthier tech diet. By the end of Week 3, put your plan into action!

WEEK 4: MAINTAIN ACTION

After some of the excitement of making a positive change wears off, you might find enthusiasm starting to wane—which is why this week is all about maintaining your family's motivation. Your family will need your support and encouragement to keep going.

Help your kids avoid people or situations that might lead them back to toxic or junk tech. If your son starts to feel he's missing out because his friends get together to game on weeknights and his goal was to game on weekends only, remind him how hard he's worked to manage his time better. Ask him whether it feels good not to be behind in school. Suggest hosting a video game tournament on a long weekend. This will give him something to look forward to, and will remind him that video games aren't out of the picture completely—he just won't be able to play them every day.

Support your family by:

- Being open to listening and validating the perceived drawbacks of the change
- Reinforcing the internal rewards of the change, including better health, connection, creativity, grades, and harmony in the home
- Continuing to motivate them towards their goals

Use the Dolphin KEYS for Motivation

You can also help to ensure your child's commitment by working on your own behaviour and communication style. Let's be honest: you're probably encountering challenges and frustrations along the way too. And although we don't mean to, sometimes we can take those frustrations out on those closest to us.

So I've developed a four-step communication strategy that you can use to enhance your child's self-motivation as they work towards making changes in their life. I introduced this approach in my previous book, *The Dolphin Parent*, where I call the method the Dolphin KEYS. I've been using it for almost twenty years, both at home and in my practice with young patients. Together, the KEYS steps comprise the essence of motivational communication.

To help you communicate more easily and effectively with your children, then, here are the four steps and how you can put them into action.

1. Kill the Shark and Jellyfish; Be a Dolphin Parent

Don't speak from a place of stress—you may try to control the situation and argue with your child (freeze and fight), and may ultimately feel overwhelmed and check out (flight). Instead, start with a few deep, controlled breaths and make sure you're calm before you begin.

Being an angry, roaring parent doesn't work in the long run. When you encounter resistance from your child, this is a signal to change your approach. As we all know, the more you push children—or anyone for that matter—the more they tend to resist. Behavioural science tells us that arguing is counterproductive when the goal is convincing someone to change. In fact, it tends to further entrench a person in their beliefs, especially a teenager.

So if you find yourself in a yelling match with your child—who's arguing that "this video game is not that bad," for example—*stop*, do something else, and come back to the issue later. Remember: the goal is not to argue. I know this sounds impossible when you're revved up on adrenalin about a particular issue. But that's precisely why you should calm down and recentre yourself before coming back to it.

To move away from the stress response to a place of inner balance, I use deep breathing (pages 118–19) and such practices as a warm bath or a walk in nature along with visualization (page 120–22). The basics, however, come first: do your best to avoid being a sleep-deprived, hungry, caffeinated, lonely, sedentary parent. Don't forget your own self-care!

2. Empathize

Express that you understand your child and that you're on their side.

We can't show love and acceptance for our kids only when they're behaving well. In fact, it's especially important to show them empathy when they're acting up. This doesn't mean that you accept problem behaviour, but it does signal that you're trying to understand the feelings and possible reasons behind it. Empathy is showing love for who your child is—bad behaviour, weaknesses, and all.

Expressing empathy to your child helps build an alliance between you—one that makes them more likely to turn to you for help when things go wrong. The acceptance you show them in tough times will also help facilitate change. And empathy has the added benefit of improving your child's self-esteem. Odds are good that when they're suffering they may be feeling alone and blaming themselves for whatever mistake they may have made. We were all children once. I'll often tell my kids that I made the exact same mistake or felt the same way they're feeling.

Here are some empathic statements you might want to try with your own kids:

- Help me understand what you're feeling.
- I can see you don't want to do your homework right now.
- I can see you're really upset.
- I can appreciate that this is really hard for you.
- I wish you could play, too.
- I don't want to break up all the fun, but it's time to set the table.

3. Identify Your Child's Goals

You're now in your child's shoes, so acknowledge their goals rather than focusing on your own.

Our behaviours are motivated by our desires—and the same is true of our children, who need to learn to connect their behaviour with their goals. Now that your child has expressed a desire to improve their tech diet and identified some SMART goals, you can remind them of these to maintain motivation.

You can also try to help them understand how their current tech consumption may be positively or negatively affecting other personal goals and values. Choose areas that matter to your child: friends, getting outside, being physically active, sleep, school, sports, and extracurricular activities.

Sometimes, though, it becomes necessary to use consequences and incentives to influence your children's behaviour. Recently, for example, I reduced my son's data usage on his phone plan because he couldn't stay under the limit. I reminded him that this had been his goal, so he understood that I wasn't punishing him but rather helping him get back on track. He knows that once he does, I'll up his data plan again. These tactics can help establish healthy habits in the short term, but the sooner you can encourage your child's internal control, the better.

4. Support Success

Express belief in your child's ability to carry out the task.

Remember, children will change when they believe something is important *and* when they feel they're capable of it. So to encourage their belief in their ability to change, try saying things like:

- I know you're capable of understanding this.
- I'm sure you'll find a way.
- I know we can work together to solve this.

As you work to proactively develop your children's self-motivation, remember that it's essential for them to believe in their ability to succeed.

How to Apply the KEYS to Specific Situations

Here are examples of how to apply the Dolphin KEYS to different situations (I've assumed that you've already completed step one and killed the shark and jellyfish). Keep in mind that these are meant to be said without control, judgment, fear, or anger, only love!

Your child went over his screen time limit: "I know it's hard to turn off your iPad when you're having fun [empathize], but your goal was to stick to your limits so that you can balance fun with schoolwork [identify your child's goals]. Come on, I know you can get back to your tech diet goals [support success]."

Your child doesn't want to stop playing video games to do homework: "I used to hate doing homework too [empathize], but you don't want to miss out on recess during school because you didn't finish your assignment [identify your child's goals]. Thank goodness you pick up things easily once you put your mind to it [support success]."

Your child resists switching to a math app because she's watching Netflix: "Aw, you look so tired today [empathize], but this is a fun way to prepare for that upcoming unit test [identify your child's goals]. You've always told me that you enjoy using the app for math [support success]."

Remind your kids that they're not alone. Check in with them often. Share your own progress—and setbacks. Come up with new ideas to help keep them motivated!

WEEK 5: MANAGE RELAPSE AND GET BACK ON TRACK

This week is all about watching for and managing any relapses by helping your kids get back on track. Research shows that motivation is dynamic; it fluctuates and tends to wane over time. So to maintain it, you need to frequently re-evaluate your efforts and find ways to boost your motivation. Think back to a time you tried a new diet or exercise regimen. How long were you able to keep it up? What got in the way of more lasting change?

At some point you may find your kids' motivation fading; they may even return to their old ways. You might hear them say something like, "It's too hard to stay away from tech during winter break. There's nothing else to do!"

Support your children by:

- Figuring out what triggered their relapse
- Coming up with coping strategies to avoid triggers
- Reviewing the benefits of change with them

You might say something like "You were doing so well. Things got better at school and you were getting along better with your dad and me. Since you also wanted more independence and money, do you want me to help you look for a part-time job?"

Decisional Balance

Rethinking the pros and cons of the change your family is making is an effective way to help family members stay motivated. So here's a motivational tool, known as a decisional balance, that can help.

Begin by asking your child to explain one of their goals to you. For example:

- Goal 1: To reduce junk tech (like gaming and social media use) and to increase healthy tech (like FaceTime or a mindfulness app)

On a blank piece of paper, draw a square (as shown below). Have your child fill in the pros and cons of changing his behaviour and of relapsing into his old ways.

DECISIONAL BALANCE

	NEW HABITS	OLD HABITS
PROS		
CONS		

Ask him to list the benefits of reducing his use of junk tech:

- More time with family and friends
- Less cranky and irritable
- More present, less distracted

What about the drawbacks? Have him list the cons involved:

- More boredom
- I just miss playing the game
- No longer able to distract myself from uncomfortable emotions

Ask him to list the benefits of going back to his old tech habits:

- It's fun for a while
- It distracts me from my problems
- I like the sense of familiarity

What about the drawbacks? Have him list the cons involved:

- I felt I let myself and my family down
- I know I can do better
- I have less time with my friends
- I'm more irritable

Have your child compare the pros and cons on the chart, and then ask: How would you rank each item out of 10 according to what's important to you? For example, if time with family and friends is very important, it would rank a 10/10. Once you do this, review the chart and ask: Are the benefits of changing your behaviour worth it?

WEEK 6: THE NEW YOU

Congratulations, you did it! This week is all about taking inventory of everything your family has learned in the last five weeks, celebrating your efforts (no matter what the results are), and maintaining good communication around tech use. This will help keep your kids on the path to a healthy tech diet.

Research shows that when we make one positive change in our habits and behaviour, it can have a ripple effect on other areas of our lives. If your kids have more time offline, they might start spending more time getting outside in nature, practising the guitar, or reading for fun. Recognize the change. Point it out. Celebrate it with a new book, tickets to a movie, a fun family room guitar playing competition, or another moderate reward.

And please remember that losing motivation and relapsing are both normal. Tell your family that studies show the average smoker has to make about seven sincere efforts to quit before it finally sticks. If you didn't get the results you wanted, be satisfied with your efforts, take a break, and try to get back on track.

Keep in mind that it takes about ninety days of daily walking on a new neural trail to develop a new habit. The neural trails associated with bad habits won't be dismantled at least till then, meaning old habits may come back at any time. So creating new habits can be messy work, with frequent slips and frustration. But don't back down or quit—keep going! Be firm and flexible as you guide your child towards their goals, and move forward together with love and positivity. In time, there's no doubt that the healthy habits will emerge. Patience, consistency, and the resiliency to get back on track are all needed.

This is a good time to re-evaluate and review your children's motivation assessment worksheets, motivation rulers, SMART goals, and decisional balances. Discuss their initial thoughts and see how things have changed. Use these tools repeatedly to discover ways to maintain and help each other meet your healthy tech goals. And remember to keep using the Dolphin KEYS for motivational communication!

Here are a few more ways to keep encouraging positive change in your children.

Use statements that foster your child's internal control: Nobody likes to be told what to do, even the children of well-meaning, intelligent, loving parents. When kids feel they're being controlled or threatened, they start to resist. The deep desire to be autonomous lies within us all.

So say things like "I can't force you to understand healthy living. I can only show you; the rest is up to you" or "I can set rules and limits in this house, but once you're off on your own, you'll be able to make your own choices."

Ask permission before giving your kids advice: Many children and almost all teenagers are resistant to unsolicited advice and suggestions, even if they're "for your own good!" Try asking your children whether they'd welcome your input before you give it. Trust me, things will go *much* more smoothly if you do.

I once had a thirteen-year-old patient named Anthony who was having trouble with some of his friends. They were picking on him and making him the butt of all their jokes. One day they posted an unflattering Instagram picture of his acne. Rather than intervening, his mom didn't say a word. But when she saw how upset he was, she said, "Anthony, sweetheart, tell me if you want to know what I would do in this situation." That opened the door for him to consider his mom's ideas, and he did eventually turn to her for advice.

Ask open-ended, nonjudgmental questions: Open-ended questions are a great way to express empathy and avoid arguments. They also go a long way towards discovering what's really going on in your children's lives. For example, one time, after my son had been at a party, I asked him whether everyone had been on their phones; he answered with an annoyed, monosyllabic "No." Not much information there! So the next time, I asked simply, "How was the party?" He said, "It was okay. I feel really bad for Jenny because someone posted a video of her on Snapchat she didn't like. And then other people wrote some mean comments about it." I explained that people often say things online that they'd never say to someone's face, which led to us talking about good online behaviour and cyberbullying.

So try saying things like "Oh, that's interesting, tell me more . . ." rather than "You should do this . . . " You'll show your kids that you're genuinely interested in their lives and aren't always trying to fix something or change their behaviour.

Change the speaking-to-listening ratio: Parents will often say to their children, "Let's talk"—and then they'll do most of the talking. That's a lecture, not a conversation! So flip the parent-to-child speaking ratio on its head and try letting your child do most of the talking. Instead of going on about how important a healthy tech diet is, ask your child to tell you why it might be important to them. Let them tell you what bothers them about social media and how they interact with friends online. When they have the space to synthesize their thoughts and express them, they're walking on the trails of change.

Tell stories: Given that we're a storytelling species, our brains and hearts respond to stories much better than they do to lectures. For example, my patient Xiao once told her son Kevin about the time she was tricked into believing a fake news story that a friend had posted online—which led to a conversation about how to evaluate authenticity and accuracy online. Later Xiao used the same approach when she told Kevin about how her mom had recently clicked on a suspicious link that led to a virus being installed in her computer. She asked him what he might have done in that situation, giving Kevin a chance to describe what he knew—and didn't know—about online security.

I truly hope and believe that these tools will help you and your family move towards not only a healthier tech diet but also a healthier life. Consuming only healthy tech, as with consuming only healthy food, isn't always easy. But now you understand the power of neuroplasticity—our unlimited ability to learn new habits and make positive change—and how to apply that knowledge. To get the most out of this information, you simply need to calm your mind, listen to your intuition, honour how you and your children are hardwired, and remember that you're at your best when you take care of yourselves, connect with others, and create from your passions. By applying the practices in this chapter and making the shift towards healthy tech, you will, in time, become better versions of yourselves.

9

A WHOLE NEW WORLD: The Next Step
in Human Evolution

*When the winds of change blow, some people build walls, others
build windmills.*

—CHINESE PROVERB

I've always wondered, *What powers human success?* And by success I
don't mean money or status, but rather a life without compromise—
one with health, security, passion, meaning, and joy. That's what I
want for my kids. And so I kept asking myself, *What are those with
passion, joy, and meaning in their lives doing differently from the rest
of us? Is it grit?* But I know people with tons of grit, and they don't
necessarily have a lot of joy in their lives. *Does it boil down to a great
childhood?* But in my practice I've been treating increasing numbers
of people who had good childhoods but are struggling with crippling
anxiety and depression, so it's not that either. *Is it persistence?
Commitment? Luck? What's the missing factor?*

Then recently I thought of my mother, whose life has been
meaningful, full of purpose. I thought of Stephen Hawking, the
cosmologist, the greatest scientist of his generation. I thought of
Lilly Singh, the comedian who emerged from depression to

8 8

conquer the cutthroat world of late night. Each was able in their own way to adapt to rapidly changing circumstances with grace. That's when I realized that, time and again, the one thing proven to lead to an awesome life is what these wildly different people all have in spades: *adaptability*.

If you've heard anything about English naturalist Charles Darwin, you're likely to remember that he developed a theory of evolution so commonly known that many simply call it "Darwinism." His study of Galapagos finches—those colourful little emblems of evolution whose beaks are variously sized and shaped to meet the needs of each particular island—showed us that all species develop through tiny, naturally selected variations. These genetic tweaks better equip a bird or a person or a cell to compete and to reproduce. The process is known, of course, as "survival of the fittest." But that phrase has led to a lot of confusion.

Some wrongly believe that Darwin was saying it's the strongest, or the most physically fit, or the most aggressive who survive. But he wasn't talking about Olympians or egomaniacs or Rambo. Nor did he mean to suggest that it was every man for himself out there, that life was a violent struggle for survival. On the contrary: "survival of the fittest" could refer to anything from the best camouflaged to the most cooperative to the cleverest. What Darwin meant was that those who thrive are the ones best suited to a given environment.

Adaptability, I've come to see, is also the factor that powers human success. So those who thrive are those who can push forward, adapt, and reinvent themselves in an ever-changing world.

Stephen Hawking himself defined intelligence as "the ability to adapt to change." And adapt he did. As he began losing mobility in his arms, the Cambridge professor developed a way of visualizing problems in his head. Some have suggested that this innovative method (remember: visualization is imaginary play) may in fact have led to Hawking's greatest discoveries. It was in this pursuit of his passions that Hawking said he found his life's purpose and meaning. Without those two guiding forces, he added, life would be empty.

Wherever you look, whether it's bacteria, plants, animals, humans, corporations, countries, or empires, it's *adaptability* that's made the difference between extinction and thriving. And today, in the age of disruption, adaptation is occurring at a faster rate than ever before. Never have we seen the speed, complexity, and scale of change we're witnessing today. Remember Blockbuster, the once-feared giant of the movie rental industry? Then along came Netflix, disrupting the idea of borrowing movies by mailing them to customers instead. A little over a decade later, Blockbuster had gone from giant killer to Chapter Nine insolvency. Then Netflix disrupted *itself*, shifting to streaming content. Now it's most noteworthy as a *creator* of content, yet another disruption.

Consider the ways you're adapting to life in the digital era compared with your parents and grandparents. Within just five years of the iPhone's 2007 launch, more than 50 percent of Americans owned a smartphone. By comparison, it took forty-five years for the mass ownership of the car to take hold, forty for the mass ownership of the radio, and almost thirty for the TV. That's why this era is so discombobulating: we've never had an innovation hit us so fast. And it's not just the iPhone—we've digitized almost every aspect of our lives, from food distribution to transport to finance. In the last two decades we've created technologies that would never have been possible with older processors. Social media, gaming, robotics, augmented reality, machine learning—the list goes on.

The problem is that these innovations are coming at us so quickly that we've barely been able to reflect on their impact. That's what's making it so hard for parents to know what to tell our children, who are drawn to new technologies as if they were coated in candy. We've had relatively little time to figure out what impact they're having on our kids' moods, behaviour, or creativity, not to mention what these new devices and apps are doing to their developing minds.

And yet equipping kids to thrive in an era of digital disruption and economic uncertainty means teaching them to be flexible and adaptable to change. That doesn't mean letting them insert any new platform or device of their choosing and then trying to figure out how it might help or hurt them. If you follow the solutions outlined in this book, they'll learn to use tech in healthy, empowering ways that will help them adapt to whatever life throws their way.

But this also means helping them learn to think critically, communicate effectively, and solve problems collaboratively. It means helping them maintain and expand their creativity and sense of contribution. These CQ skills will in turn help them respond to the raft of challenges they'll face as adults—perhaps among them job automation, climate change, food insecurity, and housing crises.

How kids connect with the world will set the course for the rest of their lives. In fact, it may help provide the answer to one of the enduring mysteries of science.

CARE, CONNECT, AND CREATE

Although we've made huge strides in understanding the human brain, it remains very much an enigma. And even what we *do* know about how to keep it healthy and strong hasn't yet translated into a consistent practice.

As I talked about in Chapter 1, brain growth began in earnest when, as our ancestors harnessed the power of fire, their energy began to be diverted from their gut to their brain. Although it is impossible to know exactly what the innovation of fire meant for early human behavior, we can speculate that humans became more courageous and creative, and our culture as we know it likely began to take shape. In order to hunt down animals and gather plants scattered across the savannah, we needed to come together and work in groups. What joy this change brought to our lives: suddenly we had friends; we started sharing ideas and stories; we developed social values. We encouraged one another; we lifted one another other up. We became increasingly creative, making art and music and dancing together. Our lives became a bit less viscerally scary and disorienting and more peaceful, meaningful, and fun.

But innovating and living together required give and take. Building alliances, maintaining loyalty, and proving our worth to other members of the tribe was a lot harder intellectually and emotionally than anything we'd done before. This stimulated further tremendous growth in our brain and nervous system.

Indeed, the latest neuroscience suggests that we didn't become social creatures because we had such big brains. Rather, it may be the opposite: our sociability could have been a major reason why our brains continued to evolve and grow larger. In time, this in turn allowed us to become even more inventive and creative.

The thing is, biologically speaking, we haven't changed much since we were hunters and gatherers. We may have Uber Eats and self-driving cars, but our brains are still programmed to function best when we're in nature, when we move our bodies, when we work together and adapt to our ever-changing environments by trying new and different ways of doing things. To our brains, it boils down to this: take care of ourselves or die; connect or suffer. And create or be left behind. This lies at the core of who we are.

When our children are deeply connected to their community, and when they're able to explore their passions and creativity and adapt to new realities, they're able to fulfill their unique potential. Doing so will flood their brains with dopamine, endorphins, oxytocin, and serotonin; it will make them feel calm, centred, joyful, worthy. This is when they're at their best. These practices will allow them to move from survival mode to growth mode. This is how they flourish.

And as it turns out, this isn't just key to healthy kids; it's also key to a long, happy life. It's taken us several millennia to pull all that together, weaving knowledge from the fields of neuroscience, psychology, and evolutionary theory, among others. The thing is, now that we finally know all that, we're often choosing to ignore it. We're allowing ourselves and our children to fall victim to devious designs engineered to keep us glued to our devices. We're multitasking in a frantic attempt to keep up. We're getting increasingly sedentary, lonely, and sick.

A NEW WORLD REQUIRES A NEW INTELLIGENCE

Despite the vast knowledge we've acquired since the Paleolithic era, our world is in a state of paradox right now, a place I call "negative evolution." We've never been so connected, and yet we've never been so lonely. Never in history have we had such convenience and knowledge at the tips of our fingers, and yet never have we been so stressed or unhealthy. Parents have never been so involved in their kids' lives, and yet we've never raised such unhealthy kids. We've made sleep deprivation a symbol of ambition and rest a sign of laziness. Parents are passing parenting over to screens. Our children aren't playing freely. They aren't bonding. Often, they aren't even looking at one another. They aren't doing the things we know they need the most. And technology presents us with another duality—between risk on the one hand and the opportunity to live our best lives on the other.

Technology has given us unparalleled access to information and has functioned as a great leveller, providing more equal access to that information. And yet rates of anxiety, depression, addiction, body image disturbance, inattention, perfectionism, and burnout keep climbing in our kids. The dilemma boils down to this: if our children don't learn to control these new technologies they'll end up being controlled by them, which will in turn make them unmotivated, unhappy, and unhealthy.

There is urgency to the task. As we enter a new era, we may begin using technology to upgrade ourselves—by implanting bionic eyes to improve our sight, for example, or by reducing mood disorders with brain embeds. Scientists are even at work designing a human brain–cloud interface that will give people instant access to vast knowledge simply by thinking. By co-evolving within a technological society, *Homo sapiens* could become *Homo technicus*, transcending current human limitations.

In some ways, that world is already a reality. We're already relying on our smartphones to make hundreds of decisions for us every day. And algorithms probably know us better than we know ourselves. Our laptops will often know when we're pregnant or have liver cancer or bronchitis long before we ever do, thanks to our search history.

Some young people are well adapted for this new world. Consider Emma González and the other survivors of the 2018 high school shooting in Parkland, Florida. Within days of the massacre that left fourteen students and three staff members dead, a group of survivors formed a roving teen advocacy group demanding change. At once innocent and savvy, the so-called "Parkland kids" rocketed to fame. They stared down powerful politicians and lobbyists who stood in the way of changing gun laws that would make schools safer. They delivered potent speeches rooted in their shared experience of terror and loss. They weaponized their social media accounts. And as a result of all that, millions heard their message. Their fury inspired national school walkouts to protest government inaction and drew more than a million protesters to their first major event, the March for Our Lives in Washington.

In González we see evidence of a new era of digital activism. The nineteen-year-old, who for a while seemed to go viral every time she opened her mouth, has an innate understanding of participatory media like Twitter, which she uses to interface with public figures like Michelle Obama. She claps back at haters and is unafraid to call out people like rapper Kanye West. Her GIF game is strong. At the lectern in Washington, she stood in silence for six minutes and twenty seconds as tears rolled down her cheeks—the same amount of time it took the gunman to commit the massacre at her school. It was a remarkable piece of political expression. That she was still a teenager who, weeks earlier, had watched her closest friends get mowed down by a gunman made it more extraordinary still.

González, it should be noted, isn't just a self-taught social media whiz. She's benefited from a Florida district school system that generously funds arts, civic, and enrichment programs. The school system she was educated in boasts a "debate program that teaches extemporaneous speaking from an early age." González was part of Parkland's renowned drama program. Her fellow survivor David Hogg, meanwhile, was part of an innovative, hands-on media training program. That's why, when Hogg found himself hiding in a closet from the gunman with a group of fellow students, he began interviewing them in order to record their reactions for posterity.

Hogg and González weren't educated in a system that emphasized standardized testing and rote memorization. Their education emphasized the CQ skills: creativity, collaboration, communication, critical thinking, and contribution. These five C's are indeed the ingredients of adaptability, and are generated in part from the P.O.D. activities I talked about earlier in the book: play, others, and downtime. Play helps us create and think critically. Others helps us learn to communicate, collaborate, and contribute. Downtime is what keeps us healthy and strong.

THE TECH SOLUTION FOR SMART, HAPPY, STRONG KIDS

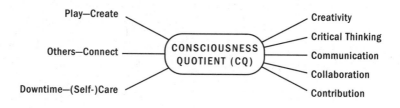

The world our children will inherit will differ radically from our own. By 2030, as they begin hitting the job market, it's predicted that some eight hundred million jobs will have been automated. And although there's disagreement over exactly which jobs are likely to disappear, economists seem to agree that it'll be the routine ones. Those who will thrive, therefore, will be those best able to wield digital tools to help them reinvent or create new jobs. And so our role as parents is to prepare them to innovate, to adapt, to be resilient to rapid change.

Traditionally, school and work were based on individual accomplishments. You went home, you wrote papers, you studied for exams. But the nature of work is changing. Today, most high-value work is being done in teams. Here's another change: until recently, the future of education was geared to the STEM subjects (science, technology, engineering, and math). That seemed the surest path to success. And for a while, it was. Increasingly, however, STEM graduates are finding it hard to get a job. Technical skills are great. But managers need people who can also communicate their ideas effectively and inspire others.

To succeed in today's highly social, ultracompetitive, tech-based modern economy, we need to help equip our children with things computers don't have—namely, the CQ skills that will help them solve unanticipated problems and cope with real-life stress. This means guiding them away from toxic tech and towards the kind of technology that fosters their creativity and reinforces their innately social natures, helping them build out their passions, their communities.

WE'RE HARDWIRED TO ADAPT AND SUCCEED

Right now we're at roughly the same place as early humans were more than a million years ago when they began learning to master fire. Whereas our primate ancestors had to figure out how to teach their children to safely handle heat, smoke, and burn, parents of the *Homo technicus* generation need to guide their children away from the tech that triggers stress and the apps, sites, and games that create dopamine-driven compulsion loops that keep them coming back for more. And just as our ancestors knew their kids couldn't be expected to manage such a dangerous tool as fire by themselves, nor should we expect our children to manage powerful technologies on their own.

The parents I meet tend to have a nuanced view of tech: they understand its power but worry about its risks. This has been true of technology for centuries—it has both excited the human imagination and provoked fears about its effects. When the earliest humans figured out how to control fire, that tool transformed all of human culture. The same thing is happening today.

The internet is knocking down many of the walls that blocked access to knowledge and so much more. Technology has improved our lives in plenty of ways, but because we're living through the chaos of transformative change, we can't fully see the other side. This can be frightening, but it's also exciting.

On top of that, tech has helped us know ourselves, to better understand our neurochemistry and how the human brain works. And when we understand how we metabolize our experiences, we can put that knowledge to work to make informed choices.

Nature gifted us neuroplasticity, granting humans the power to create new habits to help us flourish in a changing world. We can teach our children to fire and wire neural trails with healthy tech that releases endorphins, oxytocin, and serotonin. We can teach them to avoid tech that leads to the release of cortisol and to limit the stuff that dysregulates dopamine cycles. We can teach them to understand their tech consumption the way they understand food consumption. This science, and these solutions, lie within us all. They're available to anyone at any time, regardless of what anyone tells you about your child's abilities or what obstacles you may face along your life's journey. I had to remind myself of this when I received my children's diagnoses of learning disorders and when I faced my own downward spiral of illness and pain. Believe in your innate solutions—in the power of intuition, neuroplasticity, and our built-in feedback loops. Believe in the power of the beautiful, intelligent, creative human being.

If you follow the advice outlined in this book you can endow your children with the ability to use tech in healthy, empowering ways. They'll learn to adapt to whatever new tech life throws their way and to evolve with grace towards the next chapter of our evolution.

It's hard to imagine an aspect of our world that technology won't change, from politics, culture, and education to the human brain. Our paleolithic ancestors, ruminating on the changes wrought by fire, would have said much the same thing. To flourish in a changing world, our kids need exactly what they did: self-care, connection, creativity. The challenges feel new. The answers, however, are age-old. Know thyself. Love thyself. It comes down to little more than that.

THE TECH SOLUTION
by Shimi Kang, MD

As parents, one of our most important roles is to help prepare our kids to enter the world beyond the bounds of their family and community. You can influence whether digital tech becomes a force for good or for ill in your kids' lives.

Too often, we allow our kids to use tech for entertainment, not as a tool to aid in their growth and development. Remember, the habits your kids establish in childhood are the foundation for all their future behaviours. Simple things, like a good night's sleep, building downtime into their daily routines, and balancing positive tech use with real-world interactions, can have dramatic effects on how they act and feel.

Your children are innately social beings, hardwired to stay connected to their family and friends, to be curious about the people around them. Helping them to explore their passions and creativity will allow them to discover their unique potential. Connecting and creating will give purpose and meaning to their lives, and flood their developing brains with dopamine, endorphins, oxytocin, and serotonin—the happy neurochemicals!

This is when and why they feel calm, centred, joyful, worthy. This is when they are at their best. This isn't just key to healthy kids. This is the key to living a long, healthy, and happy life!

ESTABLISH HEALTHY HABITS IN THE FOLLOWING KEY AREAS:
- routine regular sleep
- balanced diet
- adequate hydration
- routine regular exercise
- routine regular play
- lots of connection and love

ESTABLISH HEALTHY TECH HABITS FOR YOUR CHILD:
- Delay! *No screens until the teens!* Or *Wait until grade 8!*
- Establish basic skills in 1) time management, 2) emotional regulation, and 3) social skills prior to introducing tech

- Teach your kids to use tech as a tool, not a toy
- Remember, if tablets and smartphones are not being used in healthy, responsible ways, you can periodically take them back
- Tech time should not be alone time
- Add tech use in after day-to-day activities rather than adding day-to-day activities in after tech use

HOUSE RULES:

- Create screen-free areas like the kitchen table, the car, bedrooms, etc.
- Create screen-free times, especially during family meals, homework time, reading, and bedtime, etc.
- Put a family charging station in an open area like the kitchen
- Turn off screens when they are not being used, including background TV
- Teach your kids to avoid screens for at least 2 hours before bedtime. Consider shutting off the Wi-Fi after 9 p.m.
- Turn off notifications and auto play on all devices in the home
- Take a digital day off
- It is natural to fall off a healthy tech diet so forgive yourself, recover, and get back on!

AVOID TOXIC TECH:

Avoid cortisol-releasing tech use that may lead to stress, addictions, FOMO, comparisons, perfectionism, multitasking, cyberbullying, social conflicts, loneliness, poor posture, prolonged sitting, sleep deprivation.

LIMIT AND MONITOR JUNK TECH:

Limit and monitor dopamine-releasing technologies like gaming and social media; watch for potential addiction.

CONSUME HEALTHY TECH:

Encourage your kids to consume tech that releases endorphins through downtime and self-care, oxytocin through meaningful connection with others, and serotonin through play and creativity.

WORKS CITED

Introduction

The data on Generation Z Jean Twenge, *iGen: Why Today's Super-Connected Kids Are Growing Up Less Rebellious, More Tolerant, Less Happy—and Completely Unprepared for Adulthood—and What That Means for the Rest of Us*, Atria Books, 2018.

1 Disruption

God only knows what it's doing to our children's brains Sean Parker, "Sean Parker Unloads on Facebook," interview conducted by Mike Allen at an Axios event, *Axios*, November 9, 2017.

48 percent of parents say that regulating their child's screen time The American Psychological Association (APA), "Stress in America: The State of Our Nation," November 1, 2017.

checking their phones 150 times a day Stephen Willard, "People Check Their Cell Phones Every Six Minutes, 150 Times a Day," *Elite Daily*, February 11, 2013.

they're spending more than seven hours a day looking at their smartphones "The Common Sense Census: Media Use by Tweens and Teens, 2019," Common Sense Media, 2019.

toddlers who spent more time in front of screens John S. Hutton, Jonathon Dudley, and Tzipi Horowitz-Kraus, "Associations Between Screen-Based Media Use and Brain White Matter Integrity in Preschool-Aged Children," *JAMA Pediatrics*, November 4, 2019.

some families have begun hiring coaches to help them raise phone-free children Nellie Bowles, "Now Some Families Are Hiring Coaches to Help Them Raise Phone-Free Children," *New York Times,* July 6, 2019.

2 Pathways

more than 40 percent of our daily activities David T. Neal, Wendy Wood, and Jeffrey M. Quinn, "Habits—A Repeat Performance," *Current Directions in Psychological Science*, August 1, 2006.

how we feel about exercise as adults Matthew Ladwig, Panteleimon Ekkekakis, and Spyridoula Vazou, "Childhood Experiences in Physical Education May Have Long-Term Implications," *Medicine and Science in Sports and Exercise*, May 31, 2018.

one-third of American workers may have to switch jobs James Manyika, Susan Lund, Michael Chui, Jacques Bughin, Jonathan Woetzel, Parul Batra, Ryan Ko, and Saurabh Sanghvi, "Jobs Lost, Jobs Gained: What the Future of Work Will Mean for Jobs, Skills, and Wages," McKinsey Global Institute, November 2017.

Children and teens age six and older "Physical Activity Guidelines for Americans, 2nd Edition," US Department of Health and Human Services, 2018.

3 Hooked

a seventeen-year-old boy from Guangzhou Liangyu, "Kings' Honor, but Whose Disgrace?," *Xinhua*, July 6, 2017.

there are 1.15 million *hikikomori* "Some Local Governments Successfully Reintegrate 'Hikkimori' Back into Society," *Japan Today*, August 23, 2019.

Facebook can identify the exact moment Darren Davidson, "Facebook Targets 'Insecure' Young People," *The Australian*, May 1, 2017.

non-screen playtime among children has plummeted Peter Gray, "The Decline of Play and the Rise of Psychopathology," *The American Journal of Play*, January 1, 2011.

Younger children now spend five and a half hours each day "Daily Media Use Among Children and Teens Up Dramatically from Five Years Ago," Kaiser Family Foundation, January 20, 2010.

How do we consume as much of your time and conscious attention as possible? Sean Parker, "Sean Parker Unloads on Facebook," interview conducted by Mike Allen at an Axios event, *Axios*, November 9, 2017.

This puts tech executives in a bind Bill Davidow, "Exploiting the Neuroscience of Internet Addiction," *The Atlantic*, July 18, 2012.

Since we've figured to some extent how these pieces of the brain that handle addiction are working Anderson Cooper, "What Is 'Brain Hacking?' Tech Insiders on Why You Should Care," *60 Minutes*, April 9, 2017.

God only knows what it's doing to our children's brains Sean Parker, "Sean Parker Unloads on Facebook," interview conducted by Mike Allen at an Axios event, *Axios*, November 9, 2017.

short-term, dopamine-driven feedback loops we've created are destroying society Amy B. Wang, "Former Facebook VP Says Social Media Is Destroying Society with 'Dopamine-Driven Feedback Loops,'" *Washington Post*, December 12, 2017.

The "ultimate freedom" is "a free mind" Tristan Harris, "How Technology Hijacks People's Minds—From a Magician and Google's Design Ethicist," *The Observer* (Britain), June 1, 2016 .

For teens the figure is more than seven hours "The Common Sense Census: Media Use by Tweens and Teens, 2019," Common Sense Media, 2019.

Adolescents are now spending more time using social media "Media Use Census," Common Sense Media, November 3, 2015.

The average child spends more time communicating through screens Ibid.

In 2008 . . . people spent an average of eighteen minutes Adam Alter, *Irresistible: The Rise of Addictive Technology and the Business of Keeping Us Hooked*, Penguin Books, 2018.

By 2019 it was up to a daily three hours and fifteen minutes Jory MacKay, "Screen Time Stats 2019," Rescue Time, March 21, 2019.

70 percent of youth with an addiction also have a mental health issue Kevin P. Conway, Joel Swendson, Mathilde M. Husky, Jian-Ping He, and Kathleen R. Merikangas, "Association of Lifetime Mental Health Disorders and Subsequent Alcohol and Illicit Drug Use: Results from the National Comorbidity Survey—Adolescent Supplement," *Journal of the American Academy of Child and Adolescent Psychiatry*, April, 2016.

36 percent of teen boys reported seeing videos Debby Herbenick, Elizabeth Bartelt, Tsung-Chieh (Jane) Fu, and Bryant Paul, "Feeling Scared During Sex: Findings from a U.S. Probability Sample of Women and Men Ages 14 to 60," *Journal of Sex and Marital Therapy*, April 2019.

53 percent of boys and 39 percent of girls thought pornography Elena Martellozzo, Andy Monaghan, Joanna R. Adler, Julia Davidson, Rodolfo

Leyva, and Miranda A.H. Horvath, "A Quantitative and Qualitative Examination of the Impact of Online Pornography on the Values, Attitudes, Beliefs and Behaviours of Children and Young People," Commissioned by the Children's Commissioner for England, June 2016.

the porn-addicted brain Todd Love, Christian Laier, Matthias Brand, Linda Hatch, and Raju Hejela, "Neuroscience of Internet Pornography Addiction: A Review and Update," *Behavioural Sciences*, September 18, 2015.

4 Stressed

85 percent of both boomers and Gen Xers Jean Twenge, *iGen: Why Today's Super-Connected Kids Are Growing Up Less Rebellious, More Tolerant, Less Happy—and Completely Unprepared for Adulthood—and What That Means for the Rest of Us*, Atria Books, 2018.

52 percent of twelfth graders Ibid.

39 percent said they often felt lonely in 2017 Ibid.

Depression in teen girls increased by 50 percent Ibid.

Suicidal behaviours in girls have increased by 70 percent Ibid.

Over the last ten years, 62 percent more girls Ibid.

For girls in the ten-to-fourteen age group Ibid.

The proportion of incoming first-year students who reported feeling "overwhelmed" Ibid.

people who spend most of their time sitting Richard Patterson, Eoin McNamara, Marko Tainio, Thiago Hérick de Sá, Andrea D. Smith, Stephen J. Sharp, Phil Edwards, James Woodcock, Søren Brage, and Katrien Wijndaele, "Sedentary Behaviour and Risk of All-Cause, Cardiovascular and Cancer Mortality, and Incident Type 2 Diabetes: A Systematic Review and Dose Response Meta-Analysis," *European Journal of Epidemiology*, March 28, 2018.

5 Wired for Health

72 percent of teenagers "Common Sense Report Finds Tech Use Is Cause of Conflict, Concern, Controversy," Common Sense Media, May 3, 2016.

the mere presence of a smartphone Adrian Ward, Kristen Duke, Ayelet Gneez, and Maarten Bos, "The Mere Presence of One's Own Smartphone Reduces Available Cognitive Capacity," *Journal of the Association for Consumer Research*, April 2017.

90 percent of undergraduates report feeling "phantom vibrations" Michelle Drouin, Daren H. Kaiser, and Daniel A. Miller, "Phantom Vibrations Among Undergraduates: Prevalence and Associated Psychological Characteristics," *Computers in Human Behavior*, July 2012.

the average human attention span shrank "Microsoft Attention Spans Online Survey," Microsoft Canada, Spring 2015.

12 percent uptick in child injuries Ben Worthen, "The Perils of Texting: Are Too Many Parents Distracted by Mobile Devices When They Should Be Watching Their Kids?" *The Wall Street Journal*, September 29, 2012.

mothers who used their devices during the meal Jenny Radesky, Alison Miller, Katherine Rosenblum, Danielle Appugliese, Nico Kaciroti, and Julie Lumeng, "Maternal Mobile Device Use During a Structured Parent-Child Interaction Task," *Academic Pediatrics*, March 2015.

perfectionism among American, British, and Canadian university students Thomas Curran and Andrew P. Hill, "Perfectionism Is Increasing Over Time: A Meta-Analysis of Birth Cohort Differences from 1989 to 2016," *Psychological Bulletin*, December 28, 2017.

mindfulness . . . improves cognitive performance D.B. Bellinger, M.S. DeCaro, and P.A. Ralston, "Mindfulness, Anxiety, and High-Stakes Mathematics Performance in the Laboratory and Classroom," *Consciousness and Cognition*, December 2015.

an eight-week training in mindfulness improved concentration John T. Mitchell, Lidia Zylowska, and Scott H. Kollins, "Mindfulness Meditation Training for Attention-Deficit/Hyperactivity Disorder in Adulthood: Current Empirical Support, Treatment Overview, and Future Directions," *Cognitive Behavior Practices,* May 2015.

Meditation improved the behaviour and self-esteem Linda Harrison, Ramesh Manocha, and Katja Rubia, "Yoga Meditation as a Family Treatment Programme for Children with Attention Deficit-Hyperactivity Disorder," *Clinical Child Psychology and Psychiatry*, October 1, 2004.

Eighty-three percent of kids from low-income families Chia-Liang Dai, Laura A. Nabors, Rebecca A. Vidourek, Keith A. King, and Ching-Chen Chen, "Evaluation of an Afterschool Yoga Program for Children," *International Journal of Yoga*, July 2015.

University students who briefly meditated Yi-Yuan Tang, Yinghua Ma, Junhong Wang, Yaxin Fan, Shigang Feng, Qilin Lu, Qingbao Yu, Danni Sui,

Mary Rothbart, Ming Fan, and Michael Posner, "Short-Term Meditation Training Improves Attention and Self-Regulation," *Proceedings of the National Academy of Sciences of the United States of America* (PNAS), October 23, 2007.

thirty times more likely to laugh Robert Provine, "Far from Mere Reactions to Jokes, Hoots and Hollers Are Serious Business: They're Innate—and Important—Social Tools," *Psychology Today*, November 1, 2000.

those who work out Gretchen Reynolds, "Even a Little Exercise Might Make Us Happier," *The New York Times*, May 2, 2018.

active people have a much lower risk Felipe B. Schuch, Davy Vancampfort, Joseph Firth, Simon Rosenbaum, Philip B. Ward, Edson S. Silva, and Mats Hallgren, "Physical Activity and Incident Depression: A Meta-Analysis of Prospective Cohort Studies," *The American Journal of Psychiatry*, April 25, 2018.

gratitude can positively affect our moods and general well-being Summer Allen, "The Science of Gratitude: A White Paper," prepared for the John Templeton Foundation by the Greater Good Science Centre at UC Berkeley, May 2018.

expressing gratitude—even if you're faking it Robert Emmons and Michael McCullough, "Counting Blessings Versus Burdens: An Experimental Investigation of Gratitude and Subjective Well-Being in Daily Life," *Journal of Personality and Social Psychology*, 2003.

6 Wired to Connect

A study of rats showed that females injected with oxytocin Ksenia Meyza and Ewelina Knapska, "Maternal Behavior: Why Mother Rats Protect Their Children," *eLife*, June 13, 2017.

a game of virtual catch Kirsten Weir, "The Pain of Social Rejection," *Monitor on Psychology*, April 2012.

Roughly one-third were "actively psychotic and/or acutely suicidal" Stuart Grassian, "The Psychiatric Effects of Solitary Confinement," *Washington University Journal of Law & Policy*, January 2006.

socially isolated people are more irritable John T. Cacioppo and Stephanie Cacioppo, "Social Relationships and Health: The Toxic Effects of Perceived Social Isolation," *Social and Personality Psychology Compass*, May 15, 2014.

when Americans were asked how many confidants they had Miller McPherson, Lynn Smith-Lovin, and Matthew E. Brashears, "Social Isolation in America: Changes in Core Discussion Networks Over Two Decades," *American Sociological Review*, June 2006.

one in three people report feeling lonely Judith Shulevitz, "The Lethality of Loneliness: We Now Know How It Can Ravage Our Body and Brain," *The New Republic*, May 12, 2013.

Fifty percent of Canadians say they "often feel alone" "A Portrait of Social Isolation and Loneliness in Canada Today," Angus Reid Institute, June 17, 2019.

Fifty percent of Americans say they "lack companionship" "New Cigna Study Reveals Loneliness at Epidemic Levels in America," Cigna Global Health Insurance, May 1, 2018.

in the U.K., 60 percent of respondents listed their *pet* Rob Knight, "New Study Reveals How Pets Are Therapeutic for Lonely, Overworked People and for Those with Little Interaction Outside of Social Media," *The Independent*, September 20, 2018.

more than a half-million people under forty who haven't left their homes "Why Won't 541,000 Young Japanese Leave the House?," CNN, September 12, 2016.

Loneliness may be worse for longevity Sharon Kiekey, "Researchers Are Working on a Pill for Loneliness, as Studies Suggest the Condition Is Worse Than Obesity," *National Post*, August 12, 2019.

Chronic loneliness has also been linked with an increased risk Javier Yanguas, Sacramento Pinazo-Henandis, and Francisco José Tarazona-Santabalbina, "The Complexity of Loneliness," *Acta Biomedica*, 2018.

being lonely increased a woman's risk of dying Julianne Holt-Lunstad, Timothy B. Smith, and J. Bradley Layton, "Social Relationships and Mortality Risk: A Meta-Analytic Review," *PLOS One*, July 27, 2010.

socially isolated kids have significantly poorer health outcomes Ayshalom Caspi, Hona Lee Harrington, and Terrie E. Moffitt, "Socially Isolated Children 20 Years Later: Risk of Cardiovascular Disease," *Journal of the American Medical Association*, August 2006.

loneliness and social isolation are major precipitants of suicide Raffaella Calati, Chiara Ferrari, Marie Brittner, Osmano Oasi, Emilie Olié, André F. Carvalho, and Philippe Courtet, "Suicidal Thoughts and Behaviors and Social

Isolation: A Narrative Review of the Literature," *Journal of Affective Disorders*, February 15, 2019.

toddlers were able to learn to clap Lauren J. Myers, Rachel B. LeWitt, Renee E. Gallo, and Nicole M. Maselli, "Baby FaceTime: Can Toddlers Learn from Online Video Chat?," *Developmental Science*, 2016.

whether Skype could help older people beat the blues Alan Teo, Sheila Markwardt, and Ladson Hinton, "Using Skype to Beat the Blues: Longitudinal Data from a National Representative Sample," *The American Journal of Geriatric Psychiatry*, March 2019.

a single friend is enough to ward off depression William M. Bukowski, Brett Laursen, and Betsy Hoza, "The Snowball Effect: Friendship Moderates Escalations in Depressed Affect Among Avoidant and Excluded Children," *Development and Psychopathy*, October 1, 2010.

Fifty-one percent of Britons said empathy has noticeably declined Robert Booth, "Majority of Britons Think Empathy Is on the Wane," *The Guardian*, October 4, 2018.

Empathy in university students is down Jamil Zaki, "What, Me Care? Young Are Less Empathetic," *Scientific American Mind*, January 1, 2011.

sixth graders who went five days Yalda Uhls, Minas Michikyan, Jordan Morris, Debra Garcia, Gary W. Small, Eleni Zgourou, and Patricia M. Greenfield, "Five Days at Outdoor Education Camp Without Screens Improves Preteen Social Skills with Nonverbal Emotion Cues," *Computers in Human Behavior*, October 2014.

the more "moral emotion"—the more outrage—a tweet contained William J. Brady, Julian A. Wills, John T. Jost, Joshua A. Tucker, and Jay J. Van Bavel, "Emotion Shapes the Diffusion of Moralized Content in Social Networks," *PNAS*, July 11, 2017.

24 percent of the teens said they'd been sexually harassed Thomas J. Holt and Andy Henion, "Identifying Predictors of Unwanted Online Sexual Conversations Among Youth Using a Low Self-Control and Routine Activity Framework," *Journal of Contemporary Criminal Justice*, 2015.

people afraid of looking bad in a partner's eyes sexted more Michelle Drouin, Jody Ross, and Elizabeth Jenkins, "Sexting: A New, Digital Vehicle for Intimate Partner Violence?", *Computers in Human Behavior*, September, 2015.

7 Wired to Create

72 percent believe children today have fewer imaginary friends Sarah Young, "Excessive Screen Time Is Killing Children's Imaginations Say Nursery Workers," *The Independent*, August 26, 2019.

inspirational lightning strikes happen only when we allow our brains to roam John Kounios and Mark Beeman, *The Eureka Factor: Aha Moments, Creative Insight and the Brain*, Random House, April 14, 2015.

8 Intuition

The Motivation Ruler Centre for Substance Abuse Treatment, "Enhancing Motivation for Change in Substance Abuse Treatment." *Substance Abuse and Mental Health Services Administration/Centre for Substance Abuse Treatment Improvement Protocols (TIP)*, No. 35, 1999.

SMART goals are goals that are George T. Doran, "There's a S.M.A.R.T. Way to Write Management's Goals and Objectives." *Management Review (AMA FORUM)*, November, 1981.

Decisional Balance Centre for Substance Abuse Treatment, "Enhancing Motivation for Change in Substance Abuse Treatment." *Substance Abuse and Mental Health Services Administration/Centre for Substance Abuse Treatment Improvement Protocols (TIP)*, No. 35, 1999.

ACKNOWLEDGMENTS

I believe we are all connected by a universal energy that can inspire us to work for the greater good. In my life I've been guided and assisted by many, and I am so grateful for the love and knowledge I've been given.

This book would not have been possible without an incredible team of people who gave it their sincerest attention and talent. First, I must thank my fearless editor Laura Dosky and gifted co-writer Nancy Macdonald. This book is infused with your big hearts and brilliant minds. It is yours to be proud of. Thank you, Nick Garrison, for bringing us together and believing in my latest metaphor! My agent, Jim Levine, you will always have my utmost respect and gratitude for opening the door to me as an author. Thank you to the teams at Penguin Random House, Levine Greenberg Rostan, and Dolphin Kids: Future-Ready Leaders who helped nurture and launch this book in record time. Thank you, Elyse Cochrane, Aman Malhotra, Justin Bains, Aanikh Kler, Amaan Kler, Joesh S. Khunkhun, and Zoravaar S. Sooch for all your insightful research, comments, and support. I am eternally grateful to my massive team of health care professionals, my mom-in-law, extended family, and caring friends who helped rebuild my body and mind after many years of disease. Dr. Joe Dispenza, Snatam Kaur, and Selina Taylor, thank you all for your gifts of love and healing.

As always, my dearest husband, Jeevan S. Khunkhun, has been my number one fan and confidant. Thank you, Jeevan, for being my light during life's darkest days. To my kids, Joesh, Jaever, and Gia: you have been the inspiration for this book. Your hugs, kisses, pure hearts, and unwavering support for your wacky mom lifted me up countless times. *The Tech Solution* was born from the concerns of parents and educators around the world who were brave enough to question and demand answers. I thank all those who do not give up on our children, no matter what everyone else is doing.

INDEX